Talk To Me In Korean
Workbook
Level 7

written by
Talk To Me In Korean

Talk To Me In Korean Workbook (Level 7)

| 1판 1쇄 · 1st edition published | 2021. 10. 6. |
| 1판 4쇄 · 4th edition published | 2024. 9. 2. |

지은이 · Written by	Talk To Me In Korean
책임편집 · Edited by	선경화 Kyung-hwa Sun, 김소희 Sohee Kim, 김지나 Jina Kim
디자인 · Designed by	선윤아 Yoona Sun, 이은정 Eunjeong Lee
삽화 · Illustrations by	까나리 존스 Sungwon Jang
녹음 · Voice Recordings by	선경화 Kyung-hwa Sun, 김예지 Yeji Kim, 유승완 Seung-wan Yu
펴낸곳 · Published by	롱테일북스 Longtail Books
펴낸이 · Publisher	이수영 Su Young Lee
편집 · Copy-edited by	김보경 Florence Kim
주소 · Address	04033 서울특별시 마포구 양화로 113, 3층(서교동, 순흥빌딩)
	3rd Floor, 113 Yanghwa-ro, Mapo-gu, Seoul, KOREA
이메일 · E-mail	TTMIK@longtailbooks.co.kr
ISBN	979-11-91343-22-9 14710

TTMIK - TALK TO ME IN KOREAN

Talk To Me In Korean Workbook
Level 7

Contents

How to Use
the Talk To Me In Korean Workbook

This workbook is designed to be used in conjunction with the Talk To Me In Korean Level 7 lessons, which are available as both a paperback book and an online course at https://talktomeinkorean.com. Developed by certified teachers to help you review and reinforce what you have learned, each lesson in this workbook contains five to seven activity sections chosen from five main review categories and 23 types of exercises.

Categories

1. Vocabulary
2. Comprehension
3. Dictation
4. Listening Comprehension
5. Speaking Practice

Types of Exercises

1. Define and Translate
2. Translation Practice
3. Fill in the Blank
4. Reading
5. Dictation
6. Complete the Dialogue
7. Matching
8. Conjugation Practice
9. Complete the Sentence

Starting from this Level 7 workbook, the Reading Comprehension category appears in a lot of lessons where you can practice reading and understanding a somewhat long piece of writing that contains what you have learned previously or in the current lesson. After reading the passage, you can answer the questions to check your understanding. Also, just like the Level 6 workbook, there are two listening categories: Dictation and Listening Comprehension. In the following Speaking Practice category, you practice speaking by repeating after the native speakers. You can download the available audio files from https://talktomeinkorean.com/audio. The files are in MP3 format and free of cost.

Lesson 1.
I see that...,
I just realized that...

-(는)구나/군요

Section I - Vocabulary

Use a dictionary to match each Korean word to its common English translation. Be sure to check out the answer before you move on to the next section and commit them to memory!

1. 부지런하다 •   • a. to be diligent, to be hard-working

2. 게으르다 •   • b. to be warm

3. 귀찮다 •   • c. to be cold

4. 차갑다 •   • d. to endure, to stand

5. 춥다 •   • e. to be hot

6. 미지근하다 •   • f. to feel cold, to be cold (in weather)

7. 따뜻하다 •   • g. to feel lazy, to be tiresome

8. 뜨겁다 •   • h. to be lazy

9. 덥다 •   • i. to feel hot, to be hot (in weather)

10. 참다 •   • j. to be lukewarm

Section II - Translation Practice

Translate each sentence into Korean using -(는)구나/군요.

11. (I just realized that) The water is very cold. (in 존댓말)

    = ~~_____~~.

12. (I just realized that) You didn't know how cold the weather in Korea is. (in 반말)

    = ~~_____~~.

13. (I can see that) This place is so big! (in 반말)

    = ~~_____~~!

14. (I'm surprised that) You are so good at Korean! (in 존댓말)

    = ~~_____~~!

15. (I just realized that) Dahye is still a university student. (in 존댓말)

    = ~~_____~~.

Section III - Fill in the Blank

Complete the dialogues by conjugating the words from Section I using -구나/군요.

16. 소희: 한 달 동안 방 청소를 안 했어? ~~_____~~!

    = You didn't clean your room for a month? (I see that) You are so lazy!

    지나: 네, 이번 달에 너무 바빠서 못 했어요.

    = No, I couldn't do it because I've been so busy this month.

    소희: 아, ~~_____~~. 내가 도와줄까?

    = Oh, (I see) You've been busy this month. You want some help?

17. 예지: 물이 미지근한 줄 알았는데, _____ !

   = I thought the water would be lukewarm, but it's so hot!

   보람: 따뜻하지 않아? 너 뜨거운 걸 잘 _____ .

   = It's warm, isn't it? (I see that) You can't take heat well.

   예지: 네, 못 참아요. 그런데 날씨가 더운 것은 잘 참아요.

   = No, I can't. However, I'm okay with hot weather though.

   보람: _____ .

   = I see.

Section IV - Reading Comprehension

Read the following journal entry. Unless otherwise noted, all words, sentence endings, and tenses have been covered in TTMIK Levels 1-6. Based on what you read, answer the questions.

내 한국 친구들은 이야기할 때 자주 "그렇구나"라고 말한다. 한국 사람들은 다른 사람의 이야기를 듣고, 항상 "아~ 진짜?", "아~ 그렇구나!" 한다. 많은 한국 사람들이 그 말을 한다. 그리고 한국 사람들은 "그랬구나!"도 많이 쓴다. 내가 오늘 힘들었다고 친구한테 말하면, 친구들이 "그랬구나"라고 말하고 나를 위로해 준다*. 친구들이 항상 내 이야기를 잘 들어 줘서 고맙다.

> * Vocabulary
> 위로해 주다 = to console

18. Choose the incorrect statement according to the journal.

   a. Korean people say "그렇구나" a lot after they listen to others.

   b. Korean people do not say "그렇구나" that much when they talk with friends.

   c. Korean people say "그랬구나" after they listen to someone talking about what happened in the past.

   d. The writer's friends say "그랬구나" when they console him/her.

Section V - Dictation

Listen to the sentences, and fill in the blanks with the missing word or phrase. The sentences will be played twice.

19. ~~_____~~ .

20. 아들: 엄마, 이거 드셔 보세요. 제가 만들었어요.

엄마: 와, 정말 맛있다! 우리 아들이 ~~_____~~ .

Section VI - Listening Comprehension

Listen to the dialogue and answer the following questions. The dialogue will be played twice.

21. Choose the correct statement according to the dialogue.

   a. 주연이는 남자의 생각보다 발이 작다.

   b. 여자는 주연이의 발이 작은지 몰랐다.

   c. 주연이는 발에 비해서 키가 작은 편이다.

22. Did the man know Jooyeon's shoe size before this conversation?

   a. 네, 알고 있었어요.   b. 아니요, 모르고 있었어요.   c. 알 수 없어요.

Section VII - Speaking Practice

A native speaker will read the dialogue from Section VI line by line. Listen and repeat one by one. You can check out the dialogue in the Answer Key at the end.

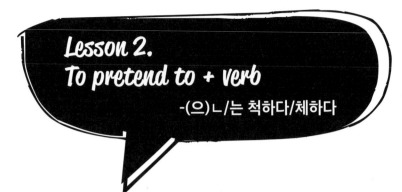

Lesson 2.
To pretend to + verb
-(으)ㄴ/는 척하다/체하다

Section I - Vocabulary

Choose the most accurate English translation from the Translation Bank, and write the alphabet next to the Korean word/phrase. Be sure to check out the answer before you move on to the next section and commit them to memory!

--- Translation Bank ---

a. to be talkative

b. to be busy

c. to come in

d. to go in, to enter

e. to come out

f. to go out, to get out

g. to be quiet, to be reticent

h. to be free, to have lots of free time

i. to hate, to dislike

j. to like

1. 말이 없다 _____ ⟷ 2. 말이 많다 _____

3. 들어오다 _____ ⟷ 4. 나가다 _____

5. 들어가다 _____ ⟷ 6. 나오다 _____

7. 바쁘다 _____ ⟷ 8. 한가하다 _____

9. 좋아하다 _____ ⟷ 10. 싫어하다 _____

Section II - Comprehension

Multiple choice. Circle the correct Korean translation.

11. I always pretend I am busy.

    a. 저는 항상 바쁜 척해요.   *b.* 저는 항상 바쁘는 척해요.

    c. 저는 항상 바쁠 척해요.   *d.* There is no answer.

12. I pretended I knew the Korean word.

    a. 저는 그 한국어 단어를 안 척했어요.   *b.* 저는 그 한국어 단어를 아는 척했어요.

    c. 저는 그 한국어 단어를 알 척했어요.   *d.* There is no answer.

13. Pretend you are working hard.

    a. 열심히 일한 척하세요.   *b.* 열심히 일하고 있는 척하세요.

    c. 열심히 일할 척하세요.   *d.* There is no answer.

14. I pretend I will go home.

    a. 저는 집에 간 척해요.   *b.* 저는 집에 가는 척해요.

    c. 저는 집에 갈 척해요.   *d.* There is no answer.

15. Don't pretend to be studying.

    a. 공부한 척하지 마세요.   *b.* 공부하는 척하지 마세요.

    c. 공부할 척하지 마세요.   *d.* There is no answer.

Section III - Translation Practice

Complete the Korean translations using -(으)ㄴ/는 척/체(하다).

16. Stop pretending to be cute.

    = _____ 그만하세요.

17. He is now pretending to be quiet, but he is actually very talkative.

    = 그 사람은 지금 _____ 지만, 사실은 굉장히 _____.

18. I was actually free, but I pretended I was busy.

    = 사실은 한가했는데, _____.

19. I didn't know the Korean word, but I pretended to know it.

    = 그 한국어 단어 몰랐는데, _____.

20. If my mom suddenly comes into my room, I will pretend to be sleeping.

    = 만약 엄마가 갑자기 제 방에 들어오시면, 저는 _____.

Section IV - Dictation

Listen to the sentences, and fill in the blanks with the missing word or phrase.
The sentences will be played twice.

21. 어젯밤에 _____. 파티에 갔잖아요!

22. 다른 사람들한테는 비밀이에요. _____.

23. _____.

Section V - Listening Comprehension

Listen to the dialogue, and answer the following questions. The dialogue will be played twice.

24. Choose the correct statement according to the dialogue.

    a. 남자는 복도에서 여자를 봤다.

    b. 여자는 남자에게 복도에서 인사를 했다.

    c. 남자는 여자에게 복도에서 인사를 했다.

    d. 여자와 남자는 오늘 처음 만났다.

25. Choose what the woman will probably say right after this dialogue.

    a. 아, 저를 봤는데 못 본 척한 줄 알았어요.

    b. 앞으로는 저를 본 척하지 마세요.

    c. 현우 씨가 복도를 청소하셨군요!

    d. 괜찮아요. 저도 못 봤어요.

Section VI - Speaking Practice

A native speaker will read the dialogue from Section V line by line. Listen and repeat one by one. You can check out the dialogue in the Answer Key at the end.

Lesson 3.
To be doable/understandable/bearable
-(으)ㄹ 만하다

Section I - Vocabulary

Match each Korean word to its common English translation.
Be sure to check out the answer before you move on to the
next section and commit them to memory!

1. 때문에 •
2. 예의 •
3. 실수 •
4. 교통사고 •
5. 덕분에 •
6. 역사 •
7. 놀라다 •
8. 추천하다 •
9. 친절하다 •
10. 죄송하다 •

• a. mistake
• b. car accident
• c. manner, etiquette
• d. to be sorry (honorific)
• e. history
• f. to be kind
• g. because of
• h. because of, thanks to
• i. to recommend
• j. to be surprised

Section II - Comprehension

Choose the incorrect English translation of the underlined Korean part.

11. 소고기 무한 리필이 19,900원이면, 그 식당 갈 만하네요.

= If the unlimited beef buffet costs 19,900 won,

_____.

a. it is worth going to that restaurant

b. I cannot wait to go to that restaurant

c. there is enough reason to go to that restaurant

12. 그 사람이 일부러 발을 밟아서 화냈다고요? 화낼 만했네요.

= Are you saying that you lost your temper because he stepped on your foot intentionally? _____.

a. It was natural for you to be angry

b. There was enough reason for you to be angry

c. You should have suppressed your anger

13. 도로에 교통사고가 났었다고요? 늦을 만했네요.

= Are you saying that there was a car accident on the road?

_____.

a. It was understandable that you were late

b. I don't understand why you were late

c. It was forgivable for being late

This time, choose the correct Korean translation of the underlined English part.

14. You said you had bumped into Hyunwoo in Paris, France? It was natural to be surprised.

= 프랑스 파리에서 우연히 현우 씨를 만났다고요? _____.

a. 놀란 만하네요   b. 놀랄 만했네요   c. 놀라는 만했네요

15. Yeji, how is your work these days? Is it okay (Is it doable)?

= 예지 씨, 요즘 일은 어때요? _____ ?

a. 한 만해요   b. 할 만했어요   c. 할 만해요

16. Did you watch the movie Seung-wan recommended? Was it worth watching?

= 승완 씨가 추천한 영화 봤어요? _____ ?

a. 볼 만했어요   b. 본 만했어요   c. 보을 만했어요

Section III - Reading Comprehension

[17~19] This passage is from the diary of Bernard, written on the day that he went to Sohee's house.

오늘 소희 집에 갔다. 소희 어머니께서 불고기와 된장찌개를 요리해 주셨다. 정말 맛있었다. 그래서 나는 소희 어머니에게 말했다. "먹을 만하네요." 그런데 소희가 말했다. "하하, 이 음식을 만든 사람 앞에서 그렇게 말하는 건 예의가 아니야. 그냥 '맛있어요'라고 하는 게 더 좋아." 나는 깜짝 놀라서, 소희 어머니에게 다시 말했다. "죄송해요. 그러니까 제 말은, 정말 맛있어요!" 그래도 실수 덕분에 새로운 것을 배워서 좋았다.

After Bernard came back home, he was curious why 먹을 만하다 could sound a bit rude sometimes, so he looked it up online. Following the result below, choose the answers for each question.

TTMIK SEARCH

| Does 먹을 만하다 sound a bit rude sometimes? | search |

Yes, it can sound rude depending on the situation.
-(으)ㄹ 만하다 means that there is enough reason or justification for a certain situation, or that something is doable or possible, but mainly in the sense of being "bearable" to do. Therefore, if you say 먹을 만하다, it means "it is edible", "it tastes okay", or "the taste is bearable".

For that reason, if you say "이 음식은 먹을 만하네요", for example, to the person who made the food, it is not a compliment at all and can sound rude.

17. Choose the correct statement according to Bernard's diary.

a. Bernard thought that the food Sohee's mom cooked was not that good.

b. Bernard made a mistake in front of Sohee's mom.

c. It is always okay to say "먹을 만하네요" to the person who cooked the dish.

18. According to Bernard's search result, which is <u>not</u> appropriate to say to the author of the book that you read?

    a. 이 책 친구한테 추천할 만하네요.

    b. 이 책 재밌어요. 인기가 있을 만해요.

    c. 이 책 볼 만하네요. 나쁘지 않아요.

19. Choose the dialogue where -(으)ㄹ 만하다 is used with the meaning of "recommendable".

    a. A: 그 책 어때요? 읽을 만해요?

       B: 네. 재미있어서 저는 잘 읽고 있어요.

    b. A: 그 사람은 정말 친절해요.

       B: 맞아요. 인기가 있을 만해요.

    c. A: 이 식당은 사람이 정말 많네요.

       B: 그럴 만해요. 이 식당이 TV에 나왔거든요.

Section IV - Dictation

Listen to the sentences, and fill in the blanks with the missing word or phrase. The sentences will be played twice.

20. 경주에 가 보셨어요? _____.

21. 어제 일을 많이 해서 머리가 좀 아파요. _____.

Section V - Listening Comprehension

Listen to the dialogue, and answer the following questions. The dialogue will be played twice.

22. Choose the correct statement according to the dialogue.

    a. 남자는 드라마 '비밀의 숲'을 싫어한다.

    b. 남자와 여자는 둘 다 드라마 '비밀의 숲'을 좋아한다.

    c. 여자는 드라마 '비밀의 숲'을 봤다.

23. A few days later, the two people had the following conversation. Which sentence can fit in the blank?

> 여자: '비밀의 숲' 봤어요? 어땠어요?
>
> 남자: 네, 봤어요. 진짜 재밌었어요!
>
> 여자: 제 말이 맞죠?
>
> 남자: _____.

    a. 네. 들을 만한 노래였어요.

    b. 아니요. 갈 만한 숲이 없어요.

    c. 네. 진짜 볼 만한 드라마였어요.

Section VI - Speaking Practice

A native speaker will read the dialogue from Section V line by line. Listen and repeat one by one. You can check out the dialogue in the Answer Key at the end.

Lesson 4.
Like + noun -같이, -처럼

Section I - Vocabulary

Match each Korean word to its common English translation.
Be sure to check out the answer before you move on to the
next section and commit them to memory!

1. 함께 •   • a. to be awkward

2. 특히 •   • b. especially

3. 대화 •   • c. each other

4. 서로 •   • d. conversation

5. 좋아하다 •   • e. together

6. 좋아지다 •   • f. to come to like

7. 느끼다 •   • g. to feel

8. 느껴지다 •   • h. to like

9. 어색하다 •   • i. to be felt

Section II - Comprehension

Decide if the Korean sentence is correct or incorrect. If it is incorrect, correct the
underlined part so that the sentence is correct and natural.

10. 강아지가 곰같은 생겼어요.

   = The puppy looks like a bear.

   ↦

11. 오늘은 일요일 같이 월요일이에요.

   = Today is a Monday (that feels) like a Sunday.

   ↦

12. 제 친구는 미국인인데 영어를 영국 사람처럼 해요.

   = My friend is American, but she/he speaks English like a British person.

   ↦

13. 바보같은 정말 그 말을 믿었어요?

   = Did you really believe that like a fool?

   ↦

14. 저같이 해 보세요.

   = Try doing it like I do.

   ↦

15. 그 사람은 한국어를 한국 사람같이 잘해요.

   = He/She speaks Korean well like a Korean person.

   ↦

16. 제가 어제 말한 것처럼 했어요?

   = Did you do it like I had said yesterday?

   ↦

Section III - Reading Comprehension

This passage is from the diary of Jill, who has been living in Korea for a while. Read the passage carefully and answer the questions.

> 한국 사람들은 '같이 하는 것'을 좋아하는 것 같다. 특히 밥을 ⊙같이 먹는 것
> 을 좋아하는 것 같다. 나도 친구들과 함께 밥 먹는 것을 좋아한다. 친구들과
> 함께 밥을 먹으면, 친구가 가족ⓒ같이 느껴진다. 나의 한국 친구들은 화장실
> 에 갈 때도 ⓒ같이 간다. 그리고 서로 기다려 준다. 처음에는 친구들과 함께 화
> 장실에 가는 것이 어색했다. 그런데 이제 나도 한국 친구들ⓔ같이, 친구들이
> 화장실에 가면 같이 간다. 나도 한국 사람들ⓜ처럼, '같이 하는 것'이 좋아졌다.

17. Choose the incorrect statement according to the journal.

    a. Korean people like to do things together.
    b. Jill does not want to be like Korean people.
    c. Jill does not feel awkward anymore going to the restroom with her friends.
    d. Jill likes to have meals with her friends.

18. Choose the group of words that have the same meaning.

    a. ⊙, ⓒ, ⓒ   b. ⊙, ⓒ, ⓔ   c. ⓒ, ⓒ, ⓜ   d. ⓒ, ⓔ, ⓜ

Section IV - Dictation

Listen to the sentences, and fill in the blanks with the missing word or phrase. The sentences will be played twice.

19. 제 친구는 _____ 한국어를 잘해요.

20. 저는 _____.

Section V - Listening Comprehension

Listen to the dialogue, and answer the following questions. The dialogue will be played twice.

* 사이 = relationship
* 차이가 나다 = there is a gap
* 지내다 = to get on

21. Choose the relationship between the man and the woman from the dialogue.

   a. 남자와 여자는 친구다.

   b. 남자와 여자는 가족이다.

   c. 남자와 여자는 같은 회사에 다닌다.

   d. 알 수 없다.

22. Choose what you cannot assume from the dialogue.

   a. In Korea, if two people are very different ages, they usually don't refer to themselves as 친구 even if they are very close.

   b. Korean people usually get along together when they are around the same age.

   c. In Korea, family members get along with each other like friends.

Section VI - Speaking Practice

A native speaker will read the dialogue from Section V line by line. Listen and repeat one by one. You can check out the dialogue in the Answer Key at the end.

Lesson 5.
As much as 만큼

Section I - Vocabulary

Choose the most accurate English translation from the Translation Bank, and write the alphabet next to the Korean word/phrase. Be sure to check out the answer before you move on to the next section and commit them to memory! Each translation is used only once.

1. 가져가다 ~~~~~~~

2. 가져오다 ~~~~~~~

3. 남다 ~~~~~~~

4. 남기다 ~~~~~~~

5. 버리다 ~~~~~~~

6. 버려지다 ~~~~~~~

7. 휴지 ~~~~~~~

8. 쓰레기 ~~~~~~~

9. 환경 ~~~~~~~

10. 보호 ~~~~~~~

Translation Bank

a. to throw away

b. to be left, to remain

c. to bring

d. to leave

e. to be thrown away

f. to take

g. trash

h. environment

i. tissue

j. protection

Section II - Complete the Dialogue

11. A: 가방이 얼마만큼 작아요?

= How small is the handbag?

B: _____ 작아요.

= It is as small as my hand.

12. A: 얼마나 가져와야 해요?

= How much should I bring?

B: _____.

= Please bring as much as you want.

13. A: 제 샌드위치에 올리브 많이 넣어 주세요.

= Please put a lot of olives in my sandwich.

B: 네, _____ 넣어 드릴게요.

= Okay, I will put this much in.

14. A: 오늘 일이 너무 많아서 두 시간 더 일했어요.

= I had so much work today that I worked two extra hours.

B: 힘들죠? 오늘 더 _____ 내일 일찍 집에 가세요.

= It's tough, right? As much as you worked more today, go home early tomorrow.

15. A: 아이가 정말 _____ 많이 컸네요.

= The kid has really surprisingly grown up a lot.

B: 네. 많이 컸죠?

= Yes. Hasn't he?

Section III - Reading Comprehension

Read the passage carefully, and answer the questions.

한국에는 무한 리필* 식당이 많아요. 무한 리필 식당에서는 먹고 싶은 만큼 음식을 먹을 수 있어요. 그런데 항상 이렇게 쓰여 있어요*. "먹을 만큼만 가져가세요.", "필요한 만큼만 가져가세요." 많은 사람들이 음식을 많이 가져가는데, 다 못 먹고 남겨요. 남은 음식은 모두* 쓰레기로 버려져요. 그러니까 환경 보호를 위해서, 음식은 먹을 만큼만 가져가야 해요.

* Vocabulary

무한 리필 = all-you-can-eat / 쓰여 있다 = to be written / 모두 = all

16. Choose the correct statement according to the passage.

    a. There are not many all-you-can-eat restaurants in Korea.
    b. People usually take a little less food than they can eat at an all-you-can-eat restaurant.
    c. You have to take just the amount of food that you will eat for the sake of the environment.
    d. There are signs that say "Take as much food as you want" at an all-you-can-eat restaurant.

17. Choose the one where the underlined part has the correct spacing.

만큼 can be used both as a particle and a noun. When it is used after nouns, pronouns, or numerals, it works as a particle; attach it to the previous word without a space. When it is used after action/descriptive verbs, it works as a noun; conjugate the verb into the modifying form so that it can modify the following word, 만큼. Either way, the basic meaning is the same.

    a. 음식은 먹을만큼만 가져가세요.   b. 무한 리필 삼겹살 만큼 좋은 것이 없죠.
    c. 사람들이 음식을 얼마만큼 남겼어요?   d. 그 식당에서는 원하는만큼 먹을 수 있어요.

Section IV - Dictation

Listen to the sentences, and fill in the blanks with the missing word or phrase. The sentences will be played twice.

18. 여기 오렌지 많이 있으니까, ＿＿＿＿＿＿＿＿＿＿＿＿.

19. A: 여기요, 휴지 좀 주세요.

    B: 네, ＿＿＿＿＿＿＿＿＿＿＿＿＿＿＿？

20. 너 밥 ＿＿＿＿＿＿＿＿＿＿＿＿＿＿＿？

Section V - Listening Comprehension

Listen to the dialogue, and answer the following questions. The dialogue will be played twice.

* 시험 = exam

21. Choose the correct statement according to the dialogue.

    a. 여자는 시험 공부를 안 했다.

    b. 여자는 시험지에 아무것도 못 썼다.

    c. 여자는 이번 시험 문제가 어려웠다고 생각한다.

22. Choose what the man is likely to say right after the dialogue.

    a. 아는 만큼 썼으면 괜찮을 거예요.

    b. 공부한 만큼 썼으니까 괜찮을 거예요.

    c. 아는 만큼 못 썼지만 괜찮을 거예요.

Section VI - Speaking Practice

A native speaker will read the dialogue from Section V line by line. Listen and repeat one by one. You can check out the dialogue in the Answer Key at the end.

Section I - Vocabulary

Translate each word into English using what you know, Talk To Me In Korean Level 7 Lesson 6, or a dictionary, then define it in your preferred language (if not English). Translations in the Answer Key are given in English.

1. 병원 (病院) = _____

2. 퇴원 (退院) = _____

3. 대학원 (大學院) = _____

4. 원장 (院長) = _____

5. 연구원 (研究院) = _____

6. 입원 (入院) = _____

7. 학원 (學院) = _____

8. 한의원 (韓醫院) = _____

Section II - Fill in the Blank

Fill in the blanks using the words from Section 1 - Vocabulary. Each word is used only once.

[9~10]

저는 한국 9. _____ 에서 일하고 있어요.

저희 10. _____ 선생님은 좋은 분이세요.

[11~13]

친구가 아파서 11. ＿＿＿＿＿＿ 에 12. ＿＿＿＿＿＿ 했어요.

3일 후에 13. ＿＿＿＿＿＿ 한다고 해요.

[14~16]

저희 아버지는 과학자세요. 그래서 14. ＿＿＿＿＿＿ 에서 일하세요.

저희 어머니는 한의사세요. 그래서 15. ＿＿＿＿＿＿ 에서 일하세요.

저도 16. ＿＿＿＿＿＿ 에서 열심히 공부해서, 나중에 교수가 되고 싶어요.

Section III - Comprehension

Choose the word that does not use 원(院) (house/institute).

17.

    a. 법원   b. 공원   c. 학원

18.

    a. 병원   b. 입원   c. 만 원

19.

    a. 퇴원   b. 회사원   c. 대학원

20.

    a. 연수원   b. 한의원   c. 원하다

21.

    a. 원장   b. 직원   c. 입원

Section IV - Dictation

Listen to the sentences, and fill in the blanks with the missing word or phrase. The sentences will be played twice.

22. 저는 _____ 갈 거예요.

23. _____ 선생님이 그렇게 _____.

Section V - Listening Comprehension

24. Listen to the dialogue, and choose the correct statement. The dialogue will be played twice.

 * 운영하다 = to run (a company, etc.)

 a. The man works for a research center.

 b. The man runs a private school.

 c. The man works for a private school.

 d. The man runs a research center.

Section VI - Speaking Practice

A native speaker will read the dialogue from Section V line by line. Listen and repeat each sentence one by one. You can check out the dialogue in the Answer Key at the end.

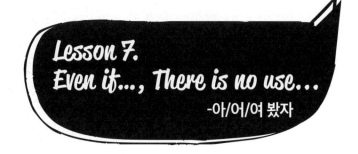

Lesson 7.
Even if..., There is no use...
-아/어/여 봤자

Section I - Vocabulary

Match each Korean word to its common English translation.

1. 미리 •   • a. to be full (in stomach)

2. 후회하다 •   • b. soccer

3. 쯤 •   • c. to be hungry

4. 낭비 •   • d. waste

5. 싸다 •   • e. to be expensive

6. 비싸다 •   • f. cake

7. 배부르다 •   • g. in advance, beforehand

8. 배고프다 •   • h. to regret

9. 축구 •   • i. approximately, around, about

10. 케이크 •   • j. to be cheap

Section II - Translation Practice

Fill in the blanks using -아/어/여 봤자.

11. Even if you call him/her, he/she will not answer.

= _____, 안 받을 거예요.

12. Even if I stay home, I have nothing to do.

    = _____, 할 일이 없어요.

13. Even if you pretend to cry, they will not fall for it.

    = _____, 그 사람들은 안 속을 거예요.

14. There is no use in regretting now.

    = _____ 소용없어요.

15. Even if you go (there) early, no one will be there.

    = _____, 아무도 없을 거예요.

Section III - Comprehension

Choose one that cannot fit in the blank of the dialogue.

16.

> 소희: 배고파요.
>
> 지나: 여기 빵 있는데, 먹을래요?
>
> 소희: 아니요. 괜찮아요. 빵이 너무 작아서 _____

a. 먹어 봤자 배도 안 부를 것 같네요   b. 먹어 봐야 배도 안 부를 것 같네요

c. 먹어 봐야일 것 같네요

17.

> 소희: 축구가 너무 어려워요.
>
> 지나: 연습 열심히 했어요?
>
> 소희: 네. 그런데 _____

a. 열심히 해야 잘 안 돼요   *b.* 열심히 해 봐도 잘 안 돼요

c. 열심히 해 봤자 잘 안 돼요

18.

> 소희: 다혜 씨는 우리랑 같이 안 가고 싶다고 했어요.
>
> 지나: 제가 한번 말해 볼까요?
>
> 소희: ~~~~~~~~~~~~~~~~

a. 그래 봤자 시간 낭비예요   *b.* 그래 봤자예요

c. 그래 봐야예요

19.

> 소희: 어제 무슨 일 있었어요?
>
> 지나: 네? 저는 아무것도 몰라요.
>
> 소희: ~~~~~~~~~~~~~~~~

a. 모르는 척해 봤자 소용없어요   *b.* 모르는 척해 봐야 소용없어요

c. 모르는 척해 봐도예요

20.

> 소희: 이 케이크 진짜 맛있네요.
>
> 지나: 맞아요. 너무 맛있어요. 이 케이크 비싸요?
>
> 소희: 잘 몰라요. 그런데 ~~~~~~~~~~~~~~~~.

a. 케이크가 비싸 봤자죠   *b.* 케이크가 비싸 봐야죠

c. 비싸 봐야 삼만 원 정도겠죠

Section IV - Dictation

Listen to the sentences, and fill in the blanks with the missing word or phrase. The sentences will be played twice.

21. _____ . 제 말은 안 들어요.

22. _____ . 비행기가 30분 후에
출발할 거예요.

Section V - Listening Comprehension

Listen to the dialogue, and answer the following question. The dialogue will be played twice.

23. Choose the correct statement according to the dialogue.

    a. 여자는 주말에 학교에 오지 않았다.

    b. 남자는 집에서 할 일이 없다.

    c. 남자는 여자와 함께 일찍 집에 갈 것이다.

    d. 남자는 지금 집에 있다.

24. Choose the sentence that does not mean the same thing as the other three.

    a. 집에 있어 봐야 할 일도 없다.

    b. 집에 있어 봤자 할 일도 없다.

    c. 집에 있어 보자 할 일이 없다.

    d. 집에 있어도 할 일이 없다.

Section VI - Speaking Practice

A native speaker will read the dialogue from Section V line by line. Listen and repeat each sentence one by one. You can check out the dialogue in the Answer Key at the end.

Section I - Vocabulary

Match each Korean word or phrase to its common English translation. All words and phrases will be used in the following sections as well, so be sure to commit them to memory!

1. 유명   •

2. 유학   •

3. 외국   •

4. 공개   •

5. 상   •

6. 다들   •

7. 드라마   •

8. 온라인 게임   •

9. 셀카   •

10. 팬   •

• a. selfie

• b. prize, award

• c. everybody

• d. foreign country

• e. famous

• f. drama

• g. studying abroad

• h. fan (person)

• i. online game

• j. making public, opening

Section II - Translation Practice

Fill in the blanks using -길래.

11. It was raining, so I bought an umbrella.

= _____ 우산을 샀어요.

12. The book was 5,000 won, so I bought it right away.

= _____ 바로 샀어요.

13. What did the man say to make you angry like this?

= 그 남자가 _____ 이렇게 화가 났어?

14. The class seemed like it was going to finish soon, so I waited.

= 수업이 곧 _____ 기다렸어요.

15. I was too tired, so I just stayed home.

= _____ 그냥 집에 있었어요.

Section III - Comprehension

Choose the one that best fits in the blank of the dialogue.

16.

예지: _____ 전화 못 받았어요?

승완: 아, 도서관이었어요.

a. 어디 있길래　　　　b. 어디 있었길래　　　　c. 어디 있겠길래

17.

예지: 왜 우산 가져왔어요? 비 안 오잖아요.

승완: ＿＿＿＿＿＿＿＿＿＿ 가져왔는데, 비가 안 오네요.

a. 비가 올길래　　　*b.* 비가 오길래　　　*c.* 비가 올 것 같길래

18.

다혜: 이번에 새로 온 선생님 수업 들어 봤어? 너무 웃기지 않아?

동근: ＿＿＿＿＿＿＿＿＿＿ 다들 그 선생님 수업 이야기만 해?

a. 얼마나 웃기길래　　*b.* 얼마나 웃긴 것 같길래　　*c.* 얼마나 웃길 것 같길래

19.

예지: 왜 의자 안 가져왔어요?

승완: 현우 씨가 ＿＿＿＿＿＿＿＿＿＿ 안 가져왔어요.

a. 가져온다고 하길래　　*b.* 가져오겠길래　　*c.* 가져올 것길래

20.

예지: 와, 사람이 정말 많아요!

승완: ＿＿＿＿＿＿＿＿＿＿ 그래요?

a. 얼마나 많겠길래　　*b.* 얼마나 많길래　　*c.* 얼마나 많았길래

Section IV - Reading Comprehension

Read the following news headlines, and answer the questions.

TTMIK NEWS

Headlines:

Article 1 >
유명 드라마 OOOO,
한국인 열 명 중에 네 명이 봤다...
얼마나 재미있길래?

Article 2 >
"한국 사람들이 온라인 게임
잘하길래..." 게임 배우려고
한국 유학 온 외국 학생들

Article 3 >
가수 OO, 셀카 공개...
"팬들이 보고 싶다고 하길래..."

Article 4 >
한국 영화 XXX이 받은
황금종려상*... 어떤 상이길래?

* 황금종려상 = Palme d'Or
(Cannes Film Festival top prize)

21. Choose the incorrect statement based on the headlines.

    a. In the headline of Article 1, after 얼마나 재미있길래, "네 명이 봤을까?" is omitted.

    b. Some students came to Korea because Korean people are good at online games.

    c. According to Article 3, the singer uploaded his selfie because his fans wanted to see it.

22. Choose the wrong guess about Article 4.

    a. It will be about the history and the power of the award in the movie field.

    b. It will be about how valuable the award is.

    c. It will be about the reason why the Korean movie XXX couldn't win the award.

[23~26] In the headlines above, you can see that people often omit the clause after -길래 when the following is obvious according to the context. Choose the awkward clause that cannot fit into the blank.

23. Article 1

얼마나 재미있길래?

= 얼마나 재미있길래 _____?

   a. 한국 드라마일까

   b. 많은 사람들이 봤을까

   c. 이렇게 인기가 많을까

24. Article 2

한국 사람들이 온라인 게임 잘하길래...

= 한국 사람들이 온라인 게임 잘하길래 _____.

   a. 한국에 돌아갔어요

   b. 한국에 오면 좋을 것 같았어요

   c. 게임을 배우기 위해 왔어요

25. Article 3

팬들이 보고 싶다고 하길래...

= 팬들이 보고 싶다고 하길래 _____.

   a. 사진을 찍었어요

   b. 팬들을 위해서 가수가 됐어요

   c. 셀카를 공개했어요

26. Article 4

어떤 상이길래?

= 어떤 상이길래 _____?

   a. 그렇게 유명해요

   b. 한국 사람들이 다 좋아해요

   c. 안 줬어요

Section V - Dictation

Listen to the sentences, and fill in the blanks with the missing word or phrase. The sentences will be played twice.

27. ＿＿＿＿＿＿＿＿＿＿＿ 그렇게 예쁜 옷을 입었어요?

28. ＿＿＿＿＿＿＿＿＿＿＿＿＿＿ ?

Section VI - Listening Comprehension

Listen to the dialogue, and answer the following question. The dialogue will be played twice.

*망원 시장 = Mangwon Market / * 엄청 = very much

29. Choose the correct statement according to the dialogue.

   a. 여자는 떡볶이가 맛있을 것 같길래 사 왔다.

   b. 여자는 떡볶이가 맛있다고 생각하고, 남자는 그렇지 않다고 생각한다.

   c. 남자는 떡볶이가 유명하다는 것을 알고 있었다.

30. Choose what the man will be likely to do after the conversation.

   a. 떡볶이를 사기 위해서 망원 시장에 간다.

   b. 여자가 사 온 떡볶이를 먹어 본다.

   c. 여자에게 떡볶이를 어디서 샀는지 물어본다.

Section VII - Speaking Practice

A native speaker will read the dialogue from Section VI line by line. Listen and repeat each sentence one by one. You can check out the dialogue in the Answer Key at the end.

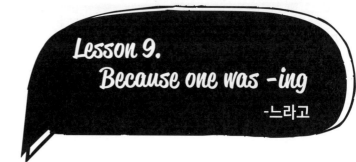

Lesson 9.
Because one was -ing
-느라고

Section I - Vocabulary

Match each Korean word to its common English translation. All words and phrases will be used in the following sections as well, so be sure to commit them to memory!

1. 준비하다 •
2. 한가하다 •
3. 정신없다 •
4. 회의하다 •
5. 힘들다 •
6. 수고하다 •
7. 샤워하다 •
8. 사과하다 •
9. 운전하다 •
10. 설명하다 •

• a. to have a meeting

• b. to be free, to not have many things to do

• c. to explain

• d. to drive

• e. to be hectic, to be swamped

• f. to shower

• g. to work hard, to make a lot of effort

• h. to apologize

• i. to prepare

• j. to be tough, to be hard

Section II - Translation Practice

Translate each sentence into Korean using -느라고.

11. I was studying, so I was busy.

    = ～～～～～～～～～～～～～～～～～～～～～～～.

12. I was getting ready, so I couldn't hear it.

    = ～～～～～～～～～～～～～～～～～～～～～～～.

13. I will be exercising, so I won't be able to pick up the phone.

    = ～～～～～～～～～～～～～～～～～～～～～～～.

14. I ate, so I spent all the money.

    = ～～～～～～～～～～～～～～～～～～～～～～～.

15. I opened the refrigerator for a little bit to look for something to eat.

    = ～～～～～～～～～～～～～～～～～～～～～～～.

Section III - Complete the Dialogue

Choose the one that best fits in the blank of the dialogue.

16.

> 현우: 오늘 한가했어요?
>
> 경은: 아니요. 손님이 와서 ～～～～～～～～～～～～.

a. 요리했느라고 정신없었어요   *b.* 요리했느라고 정신없었어요

c. 요리하느라고 정신없었어요

17.

현우: 뭐 하느라 늦었어요?

경은: 미안해요. ～～～～～～～～～～～～～～～.

a. 선물을 사느라고 늦었어요　　　*b.* 선물을 샀느라고 늦었어요

c. 선물을 샀느라고 늦어요

18.

현우: 3시에 만날래요?

경은: ～～～～～～～～～～～. 4시는 어때요?

a. 회의하느라고 안 될 거예요　　　*b.* 회의했느라고 안 될 거예요

c. 회의하겠느라고 안 될 거예요

19.

현우: ～～～～～～～～～～～? 정말 수고했어요.

경은: 힘들었지만 재미있었어요!

a. 공부했느라고 많이 힘들죠　　　*b.* 공부했느라고 많이 힘들었죠

c. 공부하느라고 많이 힘들었죠

20.

다혜: 왜 전화 안 받았어?

동근: 아, ～～～～～～～～～. 왜 전화했어?

a. 샤워하느라고　　　*b.* 샤워했느라고

c. 샤워하겠느라고

Section IV - Comprehension

Decide if the Korean sentence is correct (O) or incorrect (X).

21. 여기까지 오느라 수고하셨어요.   (O / X)

22. 비가 오느라 학교에 늦게 도착했어요.   (O / X)

23. 오빠가 집에 가느라고 제가 혼자 집에 왔어요.   (O / X)

24. 밥을 먹느라고 친구가 온 것을 몰랐어요.   (O / X)

25. 우리가 공부하느라 힘들었으니까 이제 쉬자.   (O / X)

26. 우리가 수업에 늦느라고 빨리 뛰자.   (O / X)

Section V - Dictation

Listen to the sentences, and fill in the blanks with the missing word or phrase. The sentences will be played twice.

27. 이번 한 주 동안 ＿＿＿＿＿＿＿＿＿＿＿＿＿＿ .

28. ＿＿＿＿＿＿＿＿＿＿ 핸드폰을 못 봤어요.

Section VI - Listening Comprehension

Listen to the dialogue, and answer the following questions. The dialogue will be played twice.

* 진동 = vibration

29. Choose the correct statement according to the dialogue.

    a. 남자는 전화하느라고 청소를 못 했다.

    b. 여자는 청소하느라고 핸드폰을 못 봤다.

    c. 남자는 청소하느라고 전화를 못 받았다.

    d. 여자는 전화하느라고 진동 소리를 못 들었다.

30. What is the woman likely to do right after this dialogue?

    a. 전화를 못 받아서 미안하다고 사과한다.

    b. 왜 계속 전화했는지 설명한다.

    c. 뭐 하느라고 전화를 못 받았는지 설명한다.

    d. 청소를 시작한다.

Section VII - Speaking Practice

A native speaker will read the dialogue from Section VI line by line. Listen and repeat each sentence one by one. You can check out the dialogue in the Answer Key at the end.

Lesson 10.
Sentence Building Drill #9

Section I - Vocabulary

Match each Korean word to its common English translation.
Be sure to check out the answer before you move on to the
next section and commit them to memory!

1. 해결되다 •   • a. mirror

2. 거울 •   • b. to be solved

3. 마트 •   • c. to go/come to work

4. 젖다 •   • d. to leave work

5. 걸 그룹 •   • e. to be wet

6. 들고 다니다 •   • f. to be embarrassed, to be shy

7. 출근하다 •   • g. to be irritated, to be annoyed

8. 퇴근하다 •   • h. girl group

9. 부끄럽다 •   • i. to carry around

10. 짜증(이) 나다 •   • j. supermarket, grocery store

Section II - Matching

Take a sentence fragment from column A, match it with the most appropriate fragment from column B, and write it as one sentence on the line below.

A

B

11. 과장님은 지금 회의하느라고

12. 그 친구를 만나느라고

13. 아무리 걱정해 봤자

14. 사무실이 조용하길래

15. 예쁜 걸 그룹 가수처럼

• 저도 예쁜 척해 봤어요.

• 바쁘신데, 무슨 일이세요?

• 아무도 없는 줄 알았어요.

• 저랑 못 만났군요.

• 해결되는 건 없어요.

11.

_____

12.

_____

13.

_____

14.

_____

15.

_____

Section III - Comprehension

Complete three different people's drawing diaries by choosing the most appropriate phrase from column A and matching it with the most appropriate ending from column B.

A		B
안 부끄럽다	우유가 없다	-느라고
영화배우처럼 멋있다	우유가 있다	-아/어/여 봤자
출근 준비를 하다	아무도 없다	-길래
우산을 들고 다니다	우산을 쓰다	-(으)ㄴ/는 척하다
비가 오다		-(는)구나/군요

[16~18]

16. _____,

출근할 때 집에서 우산을 가지고 나왔어요.

(= It seemed like it would rain in the evening, so I took an umbrella with me when I left home for work.)

17. _____

손이 아팠어요.

(= I was carrying around the heavy umbrella all day, so my hands hurt.)

18. 그런데 저녁에는 비가 너무 많이 와서,

_____ 소용이 없었어요.

(= However, it rained too heavily in the evening,
so even if I used an umbrella, it was no use.)

[19~21]

19. _____, 퇴근할 때
우유를 샀어요.

(= There was no milk at home, so I bought milk on
my way home from work.)

20. 그런데 집에 와서 냉장고를 열어 보니까 우유가 있
었어요. "앗, _____!"

(= However, when I came home and opened the
refrigerator, there was milk. "Oops, (I see
that) there was milk!")

21. 아침에 바쁘게 _____
우유를 못 봤나 봐요.

(= I was busy getting ready to go to work in
the morning, so I guess I couldn't see the
milk.)

[22~24]

22. _____, 혼자서 거울을

보고 있었어요.

(= There was no one in the office, so I was

looking in the mirror alone.)

23. 사실, 거울을 보면서* _____.

(= Actually, while I was looking in the mirror,

I was pretending to look cool like a movie

star.)   * -(으)면서 = while

그런데 갑자기 웃음소리가 들렸어요.

"하하하! 승완 씨, 뭐 하세요?"

24. 저는 정말 부끄러웠지만, _____.

(= Then suddenly, I heard laughter. "Hahaha!

What are you doing, Seung-wan?" I was so

embarrassed, but I pretended that I was

not embarrassed.)

Section IV - Dictation

Listen to the sentences, and fill in the blanks with the missing word or phrase.
The sentences will be played twice.

25. 그 사람이 _____.

26. _____ 않을 거예요.

Section V - Listening Comprehension

27. Listen to the dialogue, and choose the correct statement based on the dialogue. The dialogue will be played twice.

    a. 여자는 남자의 그림을 본 적이 없다.

    b. 남자는 여자가 그림을 못 그린다고 생각한다.

    c. 여자는 남자가 그림을 잘 그린다고 생각한다.

    d. 남자는 그림 그리는 것을 싫어한다.

Section VI - Speaking Practice

A native speaker will read the dialogue from Section V line by line. Listen and repeat each sentence one by one. You can check out the dialogue in the Answer Key at the end.

Lesson 11.
Making Things Happen
(Causative Verbs) -이/히/리/기/우/구/추-

Section I - Vocabulary

Match each Korean word to its common English translation.

1. 울리다 •   • a. to make someone cry

2. 안기다 •   • b. to make something melt, to melt something

3. 남기다 •   • c. to brighten

4. 앉히다 •   • d. to make someone sit, to seat someone

5. 밝히다 •   • e. to make something bigger, to grow something

6. 키우다 •   • f. to leave (food or money) remaining,
                          to leave (a comment)

7. 녹이다 •   • g. to make someone hug someone

Section II - Comprehension

The underlined parts are wrong. Correct them by using the expression given in the box. Don't change other grammar points such as tense or conjugations. The first one has been done for you.

-이/히/리/기/우/구/추-

8. 아빠가 아기를 자고 있어요. ➜ 재우고 있어요

9. 동생에게 티셔츠를 입었어요. ➜ _____

10. 선생님이 학생에게 책을 읽었어요. ➜ _____

11. 컵에 물을 좀 차 주세요. ➜ _____

12. 동생이 신발을 잘 못 신어서 제가 신어 줬어요. ➜ _____

13. 의자가 너무 높은데, 낮아 줄 수 있어요? ➜ _____

14. 책상이 너무 낮으니까 좀 높아 주세요. ➜ _____

15. 친구에게 제 남편* 사진을 봐 줬어요. ➜ _____   * 남편 = husband

16. 아이들 울지 마세요. ➜ _____

17. 음악 소리가 너무 작은데, 좀 커 줄래요? ➜ _____

18. 음식을 남지 마세요. ➜ _____

19. 엄마가 아기에게 밥을 먹어 줬어요. ➜ _____

-게 하다

20. 눈이 많이 와서 선생님이 학생들을 집에 갔어요. ➜ _____

21. 집이 너무 더러워서 친구를 못 왔어요. ➜ _____

22. 제가 좀 늦었죠? 오래 기다려서 미안해요. ➜ _____

23. 체육* 선생님이 우리를 뛰었어요. ➜ _____

* 체육 = Physical Education

24. 선생님이 저를 TTMIK 책으로 공부했어요. ➙ ～～～～～～～～～

25. 자, 공연*이 곧 시작됩니다. 가수들을 준비하세요. ➙ ～～～～～～～～～

*공연 = performance/concert

Section III - Complete the Diary

Complete the diary by choosing the most appropriate word from the box and conjugating it with the grammar point given in the parentheses. Each word is used only once.

재우다	씻기다	입히다	앉히다
먹이다	높이다	남기다	키우다

우리 가족은 엄마와 아빠, 나, 여동생이다. 고양이도 한 마리 26. ～～～～

(-고 있다). 동생은 네 살밖에 안 돼서 내가 부모님을 도와 드려야* 한다. 오늘

저녁에는 엄마와 아빠가 바쁘셔서 나와 동생만 집에 있었다. 동생을 의자에

27. ～～～～ (-았/었/였는데) 의자가 너무 낮아서 의자를 조금 28. ～～～

(-았/었/였다). 그리고 비빔밥*을 29. ～～～～ (-아/어/여 줬다). 그런데 동

생은 야채*를 싫어해서 야채를 다 30. ～～～～ (-았/었/였다). 밤 아홉 시가

되니까 동생이 울었다. 그래서 동생을 깨끗하게 31. ～～～～ (-고) 잠옷*을

32. ～～～～ (-았/었/였다). 그리고 *동화책을 읽어 주면서 33. ～～～～

(-았/었/였다).

---

* Vocabulary
도와 드리다 = to help out (honorific)   비빔밥 = bibimbap; mixed rice with assorted vegetables
야채 = vegetable   잠옷 = pajamas
동화책 = fairy tale book

Section IV - Dictation

Listen to the sentences, and fill in the blanks with the missing word/phrase. The sentences will be played twice.

34. _____ .

35. _____ .

Section V - Listening Comprehension

Listen to the dialogue, and answer the following questions. The dialogue will be played twice.

*순하다 = to be mild-mannered / * 평소 = usual day / * 침대 = bed
* 업다 = carry somebody / something on one's back / * 허리 = waist

36. Choose the correct statement according to the dialogue.

   a. 하은이는 항상 순하다.

   b. 여자는 팔이 많이 아프다.

   c. 여자는 아이를 재울 때 힘들다.

   d. 남자는 아이가 열 명 있다.

37. In which situation does the child cry?

   a. 업을 때   b. 밥을 먹일 때   c. 옷을 입힐 때   d. 침대에 눕힐 때

Section VI - Speaking Practice

A native speaker will read the dialogue from Section V line by line. Listen and repeat one by one. You can check out the dialogue in the Answer Key at the end.

Lesson 12.
Retelling/
Reporting on Speech

Section I - Vocabulary

Please define/translate each word into English. Then write it in your preferred language. (Translations in the Answer Key are given in English.)

1. 모르다 = _____

2. 염색하다 = _____

3. 물어보다 = _____

4. 덥다 = _____

5. 바쁘다 = _____

6. 형사 = _____

7. 기쁘다 = _____

8. 슬퍼하다 = _____

9. 콘서트 = _____

10. 누르다 = _____

11. 신기하다 = _____

12. 익숙해지다 = _____

Imagine that you are telling other people what you have experienced (seen, heard, found, etc.) in the past. Fill in the blanks by using -더라고(요). The first one has been done for you.

16.

생각보다 안 맵네!

나

떡볶이 어땠어?

매울 줄 알았는데
〜〜〜〜〜〜
〜〜〜〜〜〜.

친구   나

17.

공부를 열심히 하는구나.

석진   나

이번 시험에서 석진이가 1등을 했대.

그럴 줄 알았어. 석진이가
〜〜〜〜〜〜.

친구   나

18.

잘 어울리네!

나

경은

네, 빨간색이
〜〜〜〜〜

경은이가 빨간색으로 염색한 거 봤어?

나   선배*

* 선배 = senior

Read the following text, and answer the questions.

한국에 처음 왔을 때는 정말 신기한 것이 많았어요. 식당에 갔는데 식탁*에 버튼*이 있길래 그걸 누르니까 직원*이 ＿＿＿＿＿⑦＿＿＿＿＿. 너무 편리하고 좋았어요. 또 한국 사람들이 김치를 많이 먹는다는 것은 알고 있었지만, 매일 먹는다는 사실은 몰랐거든요. 여기 와서 알았어요. 친구 집에는 김치 냉장고도 있다고 해요. 그리고 거리에 카페가 아주 ＿＿＿＿＿ⓛ＿＿＿＿＿. 그때 생각했어요. '한국 사람들은 커피를 정말 ＿＿＿＿＿ⓒ＿＿＿＿＿.' 그런데 지금은 그런 것들이 신기하지 않아요. 한국에 오래 살아서 익숙해졌어요.

* Vocabulary
식탁 = (dining) table
버튼 = button
직원 = staff/employee

---

19. Choose the words that best fit in the blanks.

    a. ⑦ 오네요   ⓛ 많군요   ⓒ 좋아하는구나

    b. ⑦ 오네요   ⓛ 많더라고요   ⓒ 좋아하네

    c. ⑦ 오더라고요   ⓛ 많군요   ⓒ 좋아하는구나

    d. ⑦ 오더라고요   ⓛ 많더라고요   ⓒ 좋아하네

20. Choose what the writer came to learn in Korea.

    a. 한국 식당에서는 직원을 크게 불러야 한다.

    b. 한국 사람들은 김치를 많이 먹는다.

    c. 한국 사람들은 커피를 좋아한다.

    d. 한국에는 카페가 많지 않다.

Section IV - Dictation

Listen to the sentences, and fill in the blanks with the missing word/phrase.
The sentences will be played twice.

21. 싱가포르에 처음 가 봤는데, _____.

22. 아까 주연 씨 만났는데, _____.

23. 윤아 씨한테 물어봤는데, _____.

Section V - Listening Comprehension

Listen to the dialogue, and answer the following questions. The dialogue will be
played twice.

* 오랜만에 = after a long time

* 홍대 = Hongdae; Hongik University area in Seoul / * 글쎄 = well, maybe

24. Choose what you can learn from the dialogue.

    a. 여자는 홍대에 자주 간다.   *b.* 여자는 자주 가는 카페가 있다.

    c. 남자는 지난주에 그 카페에 갔다.   *d.* 남자는 카페가 없어진 것을 몰랐다.

25. Choose the sentence that cannot be replaced with the woman's last sentence.

    a. 오늘 보니까 없네.   *b.* 오늘 보니까 없었어.

    c. 오늘 보니까 없더라.   *d.* 오늘 보니까 없어졌던데.

Section VI - Speaking Practice

A native speaker will read the dialogue from Section V line by line.
Listen and repeat one by one. You can check out the dialogue in
the Answer Key at the end.

Section I - Vocabulary

Complete the word, and write the English translation of it. The first two have been done for you.

Matching		Translation
1. 제습 •		1. dehumidifier
2. 건조 •		2. dryer
3. 발전 •		3.
4. 전화 •		4.
5. 계산 •	• 기 (機)	5.
6. 교육 •		6.
7. 비행 •		7.
8. 자판 •		8.
9. 복사 •	• 기관 (機關)	9.
10. 세탁 •		10.
11. 선풍 •		11.
12. 언론 •		12.
13. 청소 •		13.
14. 정부 •		14.

Section II - Comprehension

Multiple Choice. Circle the best answer.

15. What is the meaning of "기 (機)"?

    a. writing, letter   b. to surpass, to go over

    c. gathering, to gather   d. frame, machine

16. "기 (機)" is not a word, but a word element. Choose the word that has the same meaning as "기 (機)".

    a. 인기   b. 기계   c. 기회   d. 기차

17. Choose what you cannot usually find in a house.

    a. 전화기   b. 세탁기   c. 자판기   d. 선풍기

18. What does "기" refer to as in 기내식?

    a. 기회   b. 기관   c. 전화기   d. 비행기

19. What is 자판기 shortened from?

    a. 자동판매기   b. 자기판매기   c. 자기장판매기   d. 자주판매기

Section III - Dictation

Listen to the sentences, and fill in the blanks with the missing word/phrase. The sentences will be played twice.

20. _____ ? 좋은데요!

21. 저희 _____ .

Section IV - Listening Comprehension

Listen to the dialogue, and answer the following questions.
The dialogue will be played twice.

22. Where is the conversation most likely taking place?

    a. At an electronics store   b. At a coffee shop

    c. In a classroom   d. In an office

23. What are they least likely to have in this place?

    a. 건조기   b. 전화기   c. 선풍기   d. 계산기

Section V - Speaking Practice

A native speaker will read the dialogue from Section IV line by line.
Listen and repeat one by one. You can check out the dialogue in
the Answer Key at the end.

Lesson 14.
No matter how...

아무리 -아/어/여도

Section I - Vocabulary

Review the vocabulary words from Talk To Me In Korean Level 7 Lesson 14 by trans-
lating the following phrases into English.

1. 아무리 어려워도 = _____

2. 아무리 비싸도 = _____

3. 아무리 맛있어도 = _____

4. 네가 아무리 바빠도 = _____

5. 네가 아무리 그게 싫어도 = _____

6. 내가 아무리 공부해도 = _____

7. 네가 아무리 부자여도 = _____

8. 직원*이 아무리 친절해도 = _____

* 직원 = staff

Section II - Complete the Sentence

Complete the sentence by conjugating the most appropriate word from the box below
with "아무리 -아/어/여도" or "아무리 -(이)라도". Each word is used only once.

비싸다	춥다	바쁘다	바보이다	많다
보다	먹다	어렵다	듣다	선생님이다

9. ＿＿＿＿＿＿＿＿＿＿＿ 부모님에게 자주 전화하려고 해요.

10. 제가 ＿＿＿＿＿＿＿＿＿＿＿ 이 정도는 알죠.

11. 시험이 ＿＿＿＿＿＿＿＿＿ 포기하지 마세요.

12. ＿＿＿＿＿＿＿＿＿＿＿ 맛있으면 괜찮아.

13. ＿＿＿＿＿＿＿＿＿＿＿ 실수할 때가 있어요.

14. ＿＿＿＿＿＿＿＿＿＿＿ 눈이 오면 기분이 좋아요.

15. 돈이 ＿＿＿＿＿＿＿＿＿ 친구가 없으면 행복하지* 않을 거야.

* 행복하다 = to be happy

16. 이 노래는 ＿＿＿＿＿＿＿＿＿＿ 좋아요.

17. ＿＿＿＿＿＿＿＿＿ 배가 안 부르네요.

18. 이 영화는 ＿＿＿＿＿＿＿＿＿＿ 지겹지* 않아. 너무 재미있어.

* 지겹다 = to get tired of

Section III - Reading Comprehension

Read the following text messages between Jina and Sohee, and answer the questions.

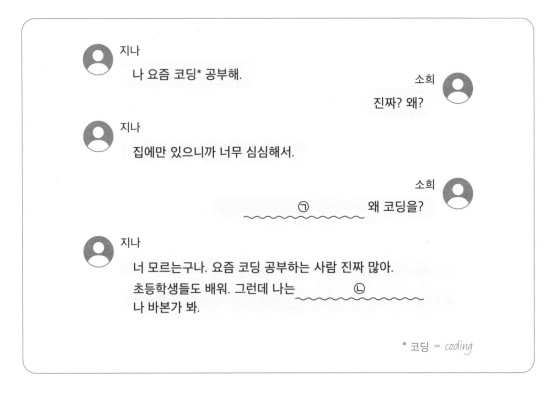

지나
나 요즘 코딩* 공부해.

소희
진짜? 왜?

지나
집에만 있으니까 너무 심심해서.

소희
ㄱ _____ 왜 코딩을?

지나
너 모르는구나. 요즘 코딩 공부하는 사람 진짜 많아.
초등학생들도 배워. 그런데 나는 ___ ㄴ ___
나 바본가 봐.

* 코딩 = coding

19. Choose the one that cannot fit in the blank ㉠.

  a. 아무리 그래도 그렇지.

  b. 아무리 집에만 있어도 그렇지.

  c. 아무리 심심해도 그렇지.

  d. 아무리 공부해도 그렇지.

20. Choose the one that best fits in the blank ㉡.

  a. 아무리 열심히 해도 어려워.

  b. 아무리 어려워도 초등학생이야.

  c. 아무리 초등학생이어도 어려워.

  d. 아무리 많아도 어려워.

Section IV - Dictation

Listen to the sentences, and fill in the blanks with the missing word/phrase. The sentences will be played twice.

21. _____ 두 시까지는 오세요.

22. _____ 공부만 하는 건 아니에요.

Section V - Listening Comprehension

Listen to the dialogue, and answer the following questions. The dialogue will be played twice.

* 심하다 = to be severe, to be too much

23. What are they complaining about?

    a. The attitude of the server   b. The location of the restaurant

    c. The taste of the food   d. The price of the food

24. What does the man think the most important thing is about restaurants?

    a. 분위기   b. 직원   c. 가격   d. 맛

Section VI - Speaking Practice

A native speaker will read the dialogue from Section V line by line. Listen and repeat one by one. You can check out the dialogue in the Answer Key at the end.

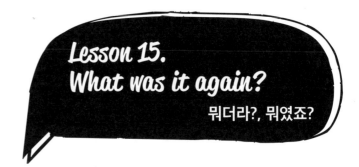

Lesson 15.
What was it again?

뭐더라?, 뭐였죠?

Section I - Vocabulary

Match the words in the Word Bank with their correct English definitions. All words and phrases will be used in the following sections as well, so be sure to commit them to memory!

Word Bank

| 생일 | 싫어하다 | 어떤 | 이름 | 약속하다 |
| 돌아가다 | 출발하다 | 끝내다 | 모든 | |

---

1. to hate, to dislike =

2. every, all =

3. name =

4. to finish =

5. birthday =

6. to depart, to leave =

7. what kind of, which =

8. to promise, to make an appointment =

9. to go back =

Talk To Me In Korean Workbook

Section II - Comprehension

Change the given Korean sentences using "-더라?", "-았/었/였지?", or "-았/었/였죠?" to suit the English translation. Level of formality should stay the same.

10. 우리 약속한 날이 언제예요?

= When is the day when we promised to meet?

↪

= When was the day when we promised to meet again?

11. 이게 한국말로 뭐예요?

= What is this in Korean?

↪

= What was this in Korean again?

12. 경화 생일이 몇 월이야?

= What month is Kyung-hwa's birthday?

↪

= What month was Kyung-hwa's birthday again?

13. 캐시가 어느 나라 사람이었죠?

= Which country was Cassie from again?

↪

= Which country did you say Cassie was from?

14. 현우 씨가 언제 한국에 돌아가죠?

= When is Hyunwoo going back to Korea?

↪

= When did you say Hyunwoo is going back to Korea?

15. 경복궁에 어떻게 가더라?

= How do you get to Gyeongbok Palace? (Can you tell me again?)

→

= How did people say you get to Gyeongbok Palace?

Section III - Complete the Dialogue

Choose the most appropriate expression to complete the dialogue.

16.

현우: 경은아, 우리 지난주에 만난 네 친구 이름이 _____?

경은: 아, 석진이?

a. 뭐였죠   b. 뭐였지   c. 누구였지

17.

현우: 우리 몇 시에 _____?

경은: 5시에 출발하자.

a. 가야 하더라   b. 갔더라   c. 갔죠

18.

주연: 우리 어디에서 _____?

경은: 회사 앞에서 보자.

a. 만나더라   b. 만날까요   c. 만났어요

19.

현우: 그 카페가 ~~~~~~~~~~~~~~~~~~~~~~~~~~?

경은: 공원 옆이잖아.

    a. 어디더라   *b.* 어디였어요   *c.* 공원 옆에 있어요

20.

다혜: 부장님, 이거 언제까지 ~~~~~~~~~~~~~~~~~~~~~~?

부장: 다음 주까지 끝내면 돼.

    a. 했죠   *b.* 했어요   *c.* 해야 돼요

Section IV - Dictation

Listen to the sentences, and fill in the blanks with the missing word or phrase. The sentences will be played twice.

21. 언제 ~~~~~~~~~~~~~~~~~~~~~~~~~~~~~~~~~~~~~~?

22. 이거 ~~~~~~~~~~~~~~~~~~~~~~~~~~~~~~~~~~~~~~?

Section V - Listening Comprehension

Listen to the dialogue, and answer the following question. The dialogue will be played twice.

*기억나다 = to remember
*바닐라 = vanilla

23. What is true about Kyung-hwa?

    a. 경화는 모든 아이스크림을 좋아한다.

    b. 경화가 안 좋아하는 아이스크림 맛은 초콜릿 (chocolate) 맛이다.

    c. 경화는 바닐라 아이스크림을 제일 좋아한다.

    d. 경화는 두 사람한테 안 좋아하는 아이스크림이 무엇인지 이야기했다.

24. Choose the incorrect statement according to the dialogue.

    a. The man has forgotten which ice cream flavor Kyung-hwa dislikes.

    b. The woman first thought that Kyung-hwa likes all kinds of ice cream.

    c. The man finally remembered the ice cream flavor that Kyung-hwa dislikes.

    d. The man and the woman know Kyung-hwa.

Section VI - Speaking Practice

A native speaker will read the dialogue from Section V line by line. Listen and repeat one by one. You can check out the dialogue in the Answer Key at the end.

Lesson 16.
I said...
-다니까(요),
-라니까(요)

Section I - Vocabulary

Match each Korean word to its common English translation.

1. 바쁘다 •   • a. to grab

2. 모르다 •   • b. to know

3. 매일 •   • c. to not know

4. 벌써 •   • d. already

5. 알다 •   • e. alone, by myself

6. 잡다 •   • f. to be busy

7. 빨리 •   • g. every day

8. 혼자 •   • h. quickly

Section II - Translation Practice

Translate each sentence into Korean by using -다니까요 or -라니까요.

9. I said I exercise every day. =

10. I said, "Do some studying!" =

11. I said I'm going to study hard starting next week! =

12. I said I really didn't know. =

13. I said come here quickly. =

14. I said I got it! =

15. I said I don't want to do this. =

16. I said I'm going by myself! =

Talk To Me In Korean Workbook

Section III - Reading Comprehension

Read the following letter, and answer the questions.

마크에게*

안녕? 편지 잘 받았어.

'-다니까(요)'를 배웠구나. 좋은 표현*이야!

그런데 이 표현은 조금 조심해야 해.

이 말을 자주 쓰면 여러 번* 말하기 싫어하는 사람 같거든.

그래서 듣는 사람이 기분 나쁠 수도 있어.

처음 보거나, 너보다 나이가 많거나, 친하지 않은 사람한테 쓸 때는 조심해.

또 모르는 게 있으면 언제든지* 물어봐.^^

그럼 안녕!

현우가

* Vocabulary

에게 = to / 표현 = expression / 여러 번 = several times / 언제든지 = whenever, any time

17. According to Hyunwoo's advice, to whom should Mark be careful of using -다니까(요)?

    a. 누나   b. 동생   c. 교수님   d. 친한 친구

18. Why do you have to be careful when using -다니까(요)?

    a. Because it cannot be used in casual situations.

    b. Because it is only okay to use it toward an older person.

    c. Because it is not often used in spoken language.

    d. Because it could sound rude.

Section IV - Dictation

Listen to the sentences, and fill in the blanks with the missing word or phrase. The sentences will be played twice.

19. 일 있어서 ~~_____~~.

20. 그럴 수도 ~~_____~~.

Section V - Listening Comprehension

Listen to the dialogue, and answer the following question. The dialogue will be played twice.

* 추석 = Chuseok (Korean national holiday)
* 기차표 = train ticket
* 예매하다 = to book (tickets)

21. What did the man likely say to the woman earlier?

    a. 나는 기차표 예매했어.   b. 나는 혼자 갈 거야.
    c. 추석에 일이 있어.   d. 내가 표를 살게.

22. What will the woman probably do next?

    a. 기차를 탄다.   b. 표를 예매한다.
    c. 기차역에 간다.   d. 부모님한테 전화한다.

Section VI - Speaking Practice

A native speaker will read the dialogue from Section V line by line. Listen and repeat each sentence one by one. You can check out the dialogue in the Answer Key at the end.

Section I - Vocabulary

Match each Korean word to its common English translation.

1. 갑자기 •   • a. to move out

2. 팔리다 •   • b. to be famous

3. 행복하다 •   • c. the last

4. 제일 •   • d. to be sold

5. 벌써 •   • e. the most

6. 마지막 •   • f. to be happy

7. 유명하다 •   • g. suddenly

8. 끝나다 •   • h. to end, to be over

9. 이사 가다 •   • i. already

10. 팔다 •   • j. to sell

Section II - Tense Conjugation

Conjugate each word into past, present, and future tense and attach the correct ending either -(ㄴ/는)대요 or -(이)래요.

	Past Tense	Present Tense	Future Tense
11. 팔다			
12. 아프다			
13. 바쁘다			
14. 춥다			
15. 유명하다			
16. 끝나다			
17. 이사 가다			
18. 없다			
19. 친구			
20. 마지막			

Section III - Reading Comprehension

Read the following diary, and answer the questions.

20XX. 01. 22.

오늘 서울에는 눈이 아주 많이 왔다. 길이 안 좋아서 버스도 늦었다. 어떤 사람들은 길이 막혀서* 집에 못 가게 되었다. 그렇지만 갑자기 내린 눈을 좋아하는 사람들도 있었다. 바로 아이들이었다. 아이들은 눈사람*을 만들고 사진을 찍었다. 어른*들은 힘들었지만, 아이들은 행복했다.

* Vocabulary

길이 막히다 = to get stuck in traffic / 눈사람 = snowman / 어른 = adult

21. What is this topic of the diary?

    a. Traffic problems in Seoul   b. The happiness of children

    c. Childhood memories   d. Heavy snow in Seoul

22. Which one is not what you would say to someone after reading the diary above?

    a. 오늘 서울에는 눈이 왔대요.   b. 버스도 안 왔대요.

    c. 길이 많이 막혔대요.   d. 아이들은 좋아했대요.

Section IV - Dictation

Listen to the sentences, and fill in the blanks with the missing word or phrase. The sentences will be played twice.

23. 주연 씨가 말한 ~~~~~~~~~~~~~~~~~~~~~~~~~~~~~~ .

24. 거기는 ~~~~~~~~~~~~~~~~~~~~~~~~~~~~~~~~ .

Section V - Listening Comprehension

Listen to the dialogue, and answer the following questions. The dialogue will be played twice.

* 연고 = ointment / * 저쪽 = (over) there / * 코너 = corner

25. What did the pharmacist probably say to the man?

    a. "그 연고는 다 팔렸어요."   *b.* "그 연고는 안 팔아요."

    c. "그 연고는 병원에만 있어요."   *d.* "병원 옆에 있는 약국으로 가 보세요."

26. Choose what you learned from the dialogue.

    a. 여자는 병원에 있다.   *b.* 약국은 문을 닫았다.

    c. 남자는 약을 못 샀다.   *d.* 여자는 필요한 것을 샀다.

Section VI - Speaking Practice

A native speaker will read the dialogue from Section V line by line. Listen and repeat each sentence one by one. You can check out the dialogue in the Answer Key at the end.

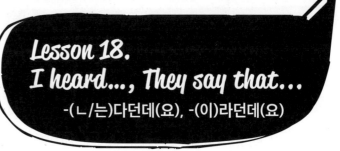

Lesson 18.
I heard..., They say that...
-(ㄴ/는)다던데(요), -(이)라던데(요)

Section I - Vocabulary

Choose the most accurate English translation from the Translation bank. Be sure to check out the answer before you move on the next section and commit them to memory! Each word is used only once.

--- Translation Bank ---

not (so) much	by oneself	laptop	to cut	later
next year	to be dangerous	new	to arrive	last week

1. 도착하다 =

2. 이따가 =

3. 혼자 =

4. 지난주 =

5. 내년 =

6. 새 =

7. 노트북 =

8. 자르다 =

9. 위험하다 =

10. 별로 =

Section II - Contraction Practice

Rewrite the following sentences in abbreviated form.
The first one has been done for you.

11. 눈이 왔다고 하던데요. ➙ 눈이 왔다던데요.

12. 머리를 자른다고 하던데요. ➙ _____ .

13. 학교에 안 갈 거라고 하던데요. ➙ _____ .

14. 대학생이라고 하던데요. ➙ _____ .

15. 여행 갔다고 하던데요. ➙ _____ .

16. 거기 위험하다고 하던데요. ➙ _____ .

Section III - Comprehension

Complete the dialogues by quoting what you heard in the past using -(ㄴ/는)다던데
or -(이)라던데. The first one has been done for you.

Section IV - Dictation

Listen to the sentences, and fill in the blanks with the missing word or phrase. The sentences will be played twice.

23. 이번 학교 축제 때 _____ ?

24. 가수는 아무도 _____ ?

Section V – Listening Comprehension

Listen to the dialogue, and answer the following questions. The dialogue will be played twice.

* 축제 = festival / * 아무도 = nobody / * 설마 = no way

25. Choose the correct statement according to the dialogue.

    a. 학교 축제에 가수가 왔다.

    b. 남자는 축제를 좋아한다.

    c. 여자는 축제에 가수가 오는 줄 알고 있다.

    d. 남자와 여자는 누군가한테서 들은 이야기에 대해서 말하고 있다.

26. How did the man feel when he heard the news from the woman?

    a. Surprised   b. Interested   c. Worried   d. Excited

Section VI – Speaking Practice

A native speaker will read the dialogue from Section V line by line. Listen and repeat each sentence one by one. You can check out the dialogue in the Answer Key at the end.

Lesson 19.
Making Reported
Question Sentences -냐고

Section I - Vocabulary

Match each Korean word or phrase to its common English translation. All words and phrases will be used in the following sections as well, so be sure to commit them to memory!

1. 물어보다 •   • a. weekend

2. 결혼하다 •   • b. age

3. 이번   •   • c. to be young

4. 시험   •   • d. to be interesting, to be amazing

5. 어렵다   •   • e. to ask

6. 어리다   •   • f. this, this time

7. 주말   •   • g. can relate, to feel empathy

8. 나이   •   • h. to be difficult

9. 공감하다 •   • i. to get married

10. 신기하다 •   • j. exam, test

Section II - Translation Practice

Translate each sentence into Korean by using -냐고.
You don't have to translate the words in the parentheses.

11. Ask (them) what time (they) will come.

    = ~~~~~~ .

12. I asked (them) why (they) didn't come.

    = ~~~~~~ .

13. (They) asked me where I was going.

    = ~~~~~~ .

14. (I) asked who said so.

    = ~~~~~~ .

15. (They) asked me how old I was.

    = ~~~~~~ .

16. Don't ask me if I'm married.

    = ~~~~~~ .

17. I asked my teacher how difficult this exam is.

    = ~~~~~~ .

18. (I) thought (he) was young, so I asked (him) if (he) was a student.

    = ~~~~~~ .

19. (I) asked my friend where she had bought the clothes.

= ~~_____~~ .

20. (My) friend asked me what I am going to do this weekend.

= ~~_____~~ .

Section III - Reading Comprehension

Read the following conversation on social media, and answer the questions.

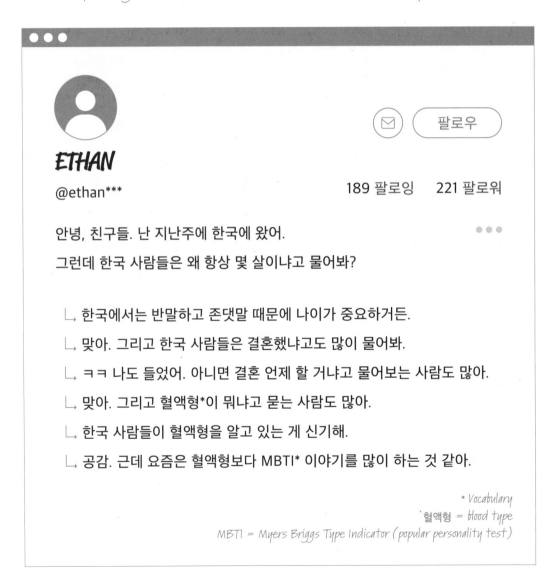

ETHAN
@ethan***

✉ 팔로우

189 팔로잉   221 팔로워

안녕, 친구들. 난 지난주에 한국에 왔어.
그런데 한국 사람들은 왜 항상 몇 살이냐고 물어봐?

⌐ 한국에서는 반말하고 존댓말 때문에 나이가 중요하거든.

⌐ 맞아. 그리고 한국 사람들은 결혼했냐고도 많이 물어봐.

⌐ ㅋㅋ 나도 들었어. 아니면 결혼 언제 할 거냐고 물어보는 사람도 많아.

⌐ 맞아. 그리고 혈액형*이 뭐냐고 묻는 사람도 많아.

⌐ 한국 사람들이 혈액형을 알고 있는 게 신기해.

⌐ 공감. 근데 요즘은 혈액형보다 MBTI* 이야기를 많이 하는 것 같아.

> * Vocabulary
> 혈액형 = blood type
> MBTI = Myers Briggs Type Indicator (popular personality test)

21. Why do Korean people ask others' age according to the conversation above?

    a. Because it determines which speech level they use.

    b. Because it determines how friendly they have to be.

    c. Because they don't want to guess how old others are.

    d. It really means nothing. It's a greeting like "How are you."

22. What question is the least likely to be asked by Koreans according to the conversation above?

    a. 몇 살이에요?   b. 무슨 일 해요?

    c. 결혼했어요?   d. 혈액형이 뭐예요?

Section IV - Dictation

Listen to the sentences, and fill in the blanks with the missing word or phrase. The sentences will be played twice.

23. _____ 물어봤어요.

24. 저한테 _____.

Section V - Listening Comprehension

Listen to the dialogue, and answer the following questions. The dialogue will be played twice.

25. Why do Korean people ask if you have eaten rice?

    a. Just out of curiosity   b. To eat together

    c. To give food   d. To say hi

26. According to the dialogue, which answer is <u>inappropriate</u> when you are asked if you have eaten rice?

    a. 네, 먹었죠.

    b. 아니요, 아직 못 먹었어요.

    c. 아니요. 이따가 먹을 거예요.

    d. 아니요. 파스타 먹었어요.

Section VI - Speaking Practice

A native speaker will read the dialogue from Section V line by line. Listen and repeat each sentence one by one. You can check out the dialogue in the Answer Key at the end.

Section I - Vocabulary

Match each Korean word or phrase to its common English translation. All words and phrases will be used in the following sections as well, so be sure to commit them to memory!

1. 태어나다 •   • a. reply

2. 복잡하다 •   • b. to be born

3. 바쁘다 •   • c. to be amazing, to be awesome

4. 먼저 •   • d. to be busy

5. 대단하다 •   • e. to forget

6. 기억에 남다 •   • f. refrigerator

7. 냉장고 •   • g. to be complicated

8. 답장 •   • h. to be memorable

9. 잊어버리다 •   • i. especially

10. 특별히 •   • j. first

Section II - Conjugation Practice

Write the sentences by conjugating the expressions
ⓐ and ⓑ with the given grammar points respec-
tively. Then translate them into your preferred
language. (Translations in the Answer Key are given
in English.) The first one has been done for you.

> ⓐ -았/었/였는데   ⓑ -더라고요.

11. ⓐ 어제 친구랑 영화를 보다

    ⓑ 사람이 정말 많다

    ↬ 어제 친구랑 영화를 봤는데, 사람이 정말 많더라고요.

    = I saw a movie with my friend yesterday, and there were so many people
      there.

12. ⓐ 그 책 읽다

    ⓑ 정말 재미있다

    ↬ _____

    =

13. ⓐ 석진 씨한테 물어보다

    ⓑ 잘 모르다

    ↬ _____

    =

14. ⓐ 냉장고 문을 열다

    ⓑ 우유가 없다

    ↬ _____

    =

ⓐ -(으)ㄴ 다음에 ⓑ -(ㄴ/는)대요.

15. ⓐ 이메일 답장하다

ⓑ 친구 만나다

↣

=

16. ⓐ 집에 가다

ⓑ 전화하다

↣

=

17. ⓐ 일 끝나다

ⓑ 영화 보다

↣

=

ⓐ 아무리 -아/어/여도 ⓑ -(으)면 안 돼요.

18. ⓐ 피곤하다

ⓑ 커피를 그렇게 많이 마시다

↣

=

19. ⓐ 날씨가 춥다

ⓑ 늦다

↣

=

20. ⓐ 바쁘다

ⓑ 그거 잊어버리다

→ ______________________________

=

Section III - Reading Comprehension

Talk To Me In Korean teacher Kyeong-eun is interviewing Cassie, who has been living in Korea for five years. Fill in the blanks by choosing the most appropriate vocabulary from the Word Bank (on the left) and conjugating it with the most appropriate grammar point from the Grammar Bank (on the right). Each word and grammar point is used only once.

Word Bank		Grammar Bank	
• 몇 살이다	• 하다	• -더라고요	• 아무리 -아/어/여도
• 좋았다	• 뭐	• -더라	• -다니까요
• 복잡하다	• 바쁘다	• -(ㄴ/는)대요	• -냐고

경은: 안녕하세요, 반갑습니다. 한국어를 정말 잘하시는데요. 어떻게 공부하셨어요?

캐시: '톡투미인코리안'이죠. 제 친구가 먼저 톡투미인코리안 책을 샀는데,
21. ~~~~~~~~~~~~~~~~. 그래서 저도 샀어요.

경은: 그렇군요. 한국어가 어렵지는 않았어요?

캐시: 음... 조금 어렵기는 했는데, 영어랑 달라서 재미있었어요. 그래서
22. ~~~~~~~~~~~~~~~~ 매일 30분은 공부했어요.

경은: 대단하네요. 혹시 한국에서 특별히 기억에 남는 일이 있어요?

캐시: 많죠. 나이 때문에 웃긴 일이 있었어요. 처음에 한국에 왔을 때, 한국 사람들이 저한테 23. ~~~~~~~~~~~~~~~~ 자주 물어봤어요. 그런데 한국에서는 나이를 다른 나라랑 다르게 계산하잖아요. 처음에는 그걸 모르고, 그... 24. ~~~~~~~~~~~~~~~~? International age가 한국어로 뭐였죠?

경은: '만 나이'요?

캐시: 아, 네! 만 나이. 그래서 저는 만 나이인 스물여섯 살로 말했어요. 그러니까 28살 친구가 오빠라고 부르라고 25. ~~~~~~~~~~~~~~~~. 그래서 계속 오빠라고 했어요. 그런데 1년쯤 뒤에 서로* 언제 태어났는지 물어보게 됐는데, 그 친구랑 저랑 같은 해*에 태어난 걸 알게 됐어요. 1년 동안 오빠라고 불렀는데, 너무 웃겼어요.

경은: 정말 재미있네요. 그래서 한국 사람이 다른 나라 사람이랑 나이를 이야기할 때는 좀 복잡하죠.

캐시: 맞아요, 진짜 26. ~~~~~~~~~~~~~~~~.

* Vocabulary
서로 = each other
해 = year

Section IV - Dictation

Listen to the sentences, and fill in the blanks with the missing word or phrase. The sentences will be played twice.

27. 어제 주연 씨를 만났는데, ~~~~~~~~~~~~~~~~~~~~~~~~~~~~.

28. ~~~~~~~~~~~~~~~~~~~~~~~~ 혼자 가면 안 돼요.

Section V - Listening Comprehension

Listen to the dialogue, and answer the following questions. The dialogue will be played twice.

29. Which one best describes the situation?

    a. The woman and the man are on the phone with Jooyeon.

    b. The woman talked to Jooyeon over the phone earlier today.

    c. The man called Jooyeon earlier today.

    d. The man is asking the woman to call Jooyeon.

30. What can you infer from what the woman said last?

    a. She has made a few phone calls.

    b. She does not want to make a phone call.

    c. She is going to make a phone call later today.

    d. She wants the man to make a phone call.

Section VI - Speaking Practice

A native speaker will read the dialogue from Section V line by line. Listen and repeat each sentence one by one. You can check out the dialogue in the Answer Key at the end.

Lesson 21.
Didn't you hear them say...
-(ㄴ/는)다잖아요/라잖아요

Section I - Vocabulary

Match each Korean word to its common English translation. All words in this section are used in the following sections, so be sure to check out the answers and commit them to memory before you move on to the next section!

1. 성공 •   • a. to contract, to sign the contract

2. 실패 •   • b. slowly

3. 실수 •   • c. of course, naturally

4. 집주인 •   • d. reply (on internet)

5. 계약하다 •   • e. to be wrong

6. 당연히 •   • f. mistake

7. 천천히 •   • g. success

8. 급하다 •   • h. failure

9. 틀리다 •   • i. to be urgent

10. 답글 •   • j. landlord

Section II - Conjugation Practice

Translate English sentences by attaching either -잖아요 or -다잖아요/라잖아요 to the given sentence.

[11~12]

Dahye goes to the bookstore. = 다혜 씨가 서점에 가요.

11. Come on, Dahye is going to the bookstore. = _____.

12. Don't you hear Dahye saying that she is going to the bookstore?

    = _____.

[13~14]

It was rainy outside. = 밖에 비가 오고 있었어요.

13. Come on, it was raining outside. = _____.

14. Don't you hear them saying it was raining outside?

    = _____.

[15~16]

These are Sukjun's clothes. = 이거 석준 씨 옷이에요.

15. Come on, these are Sukjun's clothes. = _____.

16. Don't you hear them saying that these are Sukjun's clothes?

    = _____.

[17~18]

Sohee's birthday is this Saturday. = 소희 씨 생일이 이번 주 토요일이에요.

17. Come on, Sohee's birthday is this Saturday. = _____.

18. Don't you hear them saying that Sohee's birthday is this Saturday?

    = _____.

[19~20]

That was 10 years ago. = 그건 10년 전이었어요.

19. Come on, that was 10 years ago. = _____.

20. Don't you hear them saying that was 10 years ago?

= _____.

Section III - Reading Comprehension

On the TTMIK counseling center website, people posted their problems. Give them solutions by attaching -다잖아요/라잖아요 to the most appropriate saying from the list below.

--- **Wise Sayings** ---

- 노력하면 못 할 것이 없다
  If you make the effort, there is nothing you can't do.

- 시간은 기다려 주지 않는다
  Time waits for no one.

- 실패는 성공의 어머니
  Failure is the mother of success.

- 급할수록 천천히 가라
  More haste, less speed.

● ● ●

TTMIK 고민 상담소
TTMIK Counseling Center

21.

안녕하세요! 저는 한국어를 배우고 있는 학생이에요. 제가 한국어를 2년 동안 배웠는데요. 한국어로 말할 때 아직도 많이 틀려요. ㅠ_ㅠ 어떻게 하면 실수를 안 할 수 있을까요? 진짜 한국어 잘하고 싶어요!!!!

답글   ↳ daniel.0610: 와, 한국어 잘하시네요!!! ^0^

        ↳ thisisyou: 실수해도 괜찮아요! _____ .

            실수를 많이 할수록 많이 배울 거예요.

22.

저는 스물여덟 여자입니다. 이번에 새로운 회사에서 일하게 됐어요.

그래서 회사에서 가까운 집으로 이사하기 위해서 알아보고 있어요.

그런데 그 중 한 집의 집주인이 빨리 계약하자고 해서 마음이 급해요.

빨리 계약하는 것이 좋을까요?

답글   ↳ thisisyou: 저는 천천히 하는 게 좋을 것 같아요!

            _____ .

        ↳ nicerrrr: 좋은 방이면 빨리 계약하세요. 다른 사람이 먼저

            계약할 수도 있어요.

        ↳ coco_5: 천천히 생각해 보고 결정하세요.

23.

저는 고등학생 남자예요.

저는 많은 언어를 배우고 싶은데요. 지금은 영어만 배워도 너무 어려워요.

그래도 언어를 5개 정도 배우고 싶어요. 할 수 있을까요?

답글   ↳ nerdynerd._.: 저는 언어를 3개 공부했는데, 정말 어려웠어요!

            ㅠ_ㅠ 힘내요!

        ↳ thisisyou: 네, 당연히 할 수 있죠! _____ .

        ↳ love.237: 어떤 언어를 공부하실 거예요?

Section IV - Dictation

Listen to the sentences, and fill in the blanks with the missing word or phrase. The sentences will be played twice.

24. 커피보다 차가 ~~~~~~~~~~~~~~~~~~~~~~~~~~~~~~~~~~~~ .

25. ~~~~~~~~~~~~~~~~~~ 사람이 현우 씨 ~~~~~~~~~~~~~ .

Section V - Listening Comprehension

26. Listen to the dialogue, and choose the correct statement based on the dialogue. The dialogue will be played twice.

    a. 캐시 씨는 점심을 다 같이 먹고 싶어 한다.

    b. 캐시 씨는 남자랑 점심을 같이 먹는 것이 싫다고 말했다.

    c. 캐시 씨는 점심을 혼자 먹겠다고 말했다.

    d. 캐시 씨는 점심을 이미 먹었다.

Section VI - Speaking Practice

A native speaker will read the dialogue from Section V line by line. Listen and repeat each sentence one by one. You can check out the dialogue in the Answer Key at the end.

Section I - Vocabulary

Match each Korean word to its common English translation.

1. 결정 (決定) •   • a. particular, specific

2. 인정 (認定) •   • b. setting, set-up

3. 예정 (豫定) •   • c. formal, legal

4. 확정 (確定) •   • d. fixed member, capacity

5. 일정 (一定) •   • e. periodical, regular

6. 특정 (特定) •   • f. decision

7. 판정 (判定) •   • g. scheduling, planning

8. 설정 (設定) •   • h. fixation, fastening

9. 가정 (假定) •   • i. supposition, assumption

10. 정원 (定員) •   • j. stability, calm

11. 안정 (安定) •   • k. admitting, approval

12. 정기 (定期) •   • l. judgement, decision

13. 정식 (定式) •   • m. fixed price, official price

14. 정가 (定價) •   • n. fixed, regular, constant

15. 고정 (固定) •   • o. confirmation, finalization

Section II - Comprehension

Choose the word that best fits in the blank.

16. 뭐 먹을래? 네가 _____ 해.

      a. 안정   *b.* 결정   *c.* 고정   *d.* 가정

17. 우리 비행기는 곧 인천 공항(Incheon International Airport)에 도착할
_____ 입니다.

      a. 예정   *b.* 확정   *c.* 특정   *d.* 정가

18. 많이 놀랐죠? 좀 _____ 을 취하세요.

      a. 가정   *b.* 안정   *c.* 인정   *d.* 일정

19. 저는 매일 _____ 한 시간에 일어나요.

      a. 고정   *b.* 정기   *c.* 일정   *d.* 판정

20. 내가 잘못했어. _____ 할게. 미안해.

      a. 인정   *b.* 가정   *c.* 설정   *d.* 정원

Section III - Fill in the Blank

The following are rap lyrics that rhyme with words that use 정(定). Fill in the blanks using the words in Section I. Each word is used only once and as a noun without -하다.

Yo, 안녕. 21. _____ 으로 날 소개할게 모두 채널 고정*
나는 지금부터 한국어로 랩을 할 22. _____

어떤 단어를 쓸까? 정말 어려운 23. _____

많은 단어를 보고 생각 그리고 확정

내 랩을 듣자마자 너는 마음이 24. _____

그리고 내가 최고인 걸 25. _____ yeah.

네가 아무리 열심히 해도 나는 26. _____ 승~

* 채널 고정 = (lit. channel fixation) stay tuned

Section IV - Dictation

Listen to the sentences, and fill in the blanks with the missing word or phrase. The sentences will be played twice.

27. 이 식당은 10년 동안 _____ .

28. 이 옷은 _____ 세일하고 있어요.

Section V - Listening Comprehension

True/False - Listen to the dialogue, and decide if each statement is true or false. Write T if the statement is true, and write F if it is not. The dialogue will be played twice.

* 세일하다 = to be on sale

29. The man has not decided what to buy yet. _____

30. The clothing item they are talking about is being offered at a special price. _____

Section VI - Speaking Practice

A native speaker will read the dialogue from Section V line by line. Listen and repeat each sentence one by one. You can check out the dialogue in the Answer Key at the end.

Lesson 23.
No matter whether you do it or not -(으)나 마나

Section I - Vocabulary

Use a dictionary to match each Korean word to its common
English translation. Be sure to check out the answer before
you move on to the next section and commit them to memory!

1. 뻔하다 •   • a. to lose

2. 이기다 •   • b. content

3. 지다 •   • c. excuse

4. 내용 •   • d. properly, right

5. 변명 •   • e. obviously, of course

6. 제대로 •   • f. to be thin

7. 더럽다 •   • g. to be dirty

8. 당연히 •   • h. usual day

9. 얇다 •   • i. to be obvious, predictable

10. 평소 •   • j. to win

Section II - Comprehension

Complete the translations. Each sentence uses -(으)나 마나 once.

11. Whether you ask them or not, they will certainly say they will be late.

= _____ 늦는다고 _____ .

12. No matter whether you talk to him or not, it will be the same.

= _____ 똑같을 거예요.

13. No need to see the movie. The story is predictable.

= 그 영화 _____ . 내용이 뻔해요.

14. No need to see, Kyung-hwa will win.

= _____ 경화 씨가 _____ .

15. Whether I do it diligently or not, it will be the same.

= 제가 _____ .

Section III - Complete the Dialogue

Complete the dialogues using -(으)나 마나.

16. A: 현우 씨 이야기 들어 봤어요?

B: 아니요. _____

변명만 할 것 같아요.

17. A: 이 방 제가 청소할게요.

B: 하지 마세요. _____ 더러울 거예요.

18.   A: 추우면 이 옷 입어요.

      B: 이 옷이요? 너무 얇아서 ~~~~~~~~~~~~~~~~~~~~~~~~~~~ 것 같아요.

19.   A: 이 옷 입어 볼래요?

      B: 아니요. ~~~~~~~~~~~~~~~~~~~~~~~ 딱* 맞을 것 같아요.

* 딱 = just, exactly

20. A: 그 식당 지금쯤 문 닫았을까요? 전화해 볼까요?

      B: ~~~~~~~~~~~~~~~~~~~~~~~~~~~~~. 10시인데 당연히 닫았죠.

Section IV - Dictation

Listen to the sentences, and fill in the blanks with the missing word or phrase. The sentences will be played twice.

21. 콜라를 그렇게 ~~~~~~~~~~~~~~~~~~~~~~~~~~~~~.

22. 저는 화장을 ~~~~~~~~~~~~~~~~~~~~~~~~~~~~~ . .

Section V - Listening Comprehension

Listen to the dialogue, and answer the following question.
The dialogue will be played twice.

* 볼링 = bowling
* 시합하다 = to have a match
* 내기하다 = to make a bet

23. Choose what you can learn from the dialogue.

      a. 주연 씨는 평소에 볼링 시합에서 자주 이긴다.

      b. 여자는 주연 씨가 볼링 시합에서 질 것이라고 생각한다.

      c. 남자는 주연 씨가 볼링 시합에서 이길 것이라고 생각한다.

      d. 여자는 볼링을 좋아한다.

24. Choose the sentence that cannot fit in the blank.

남자: 주연 씨가 일 등 못 할 수도 있죠. 내기해요.

여자: _____ .

a. 내기하나 마나 주연 씨가 이길 거예요.

b. 볼링 시합을 하나 마나예요.

c. 주연 씨가 일 등을 하나 마나예요.

d. 해 보나 마나예요.

Section VI - Speaking Practice

A native speaker will read the dialogue from Section V line by line. Listen and repeat each sentence one by one. You can check out the dialogue in the Answer Key at the end.

Lesson 24.
To have been put into a certain state

Passive Voice + -어 있다

Section I - Vocabulary

Use a dictionary to match each Korean word to its common English translation. All words are used in the following sections, so be sure to check out the answer before you move on to the next section and commit them to memory!

1. 책상 •   • a. police station

2. 의자 •   • b. to be placed in a basket/bag

3. 컵 •   • c. desk

4. 바닥 •   • d. floor

5. 어둡다 •   • e. basket

6. 도둑 •   • f. chair

7. 경찰서 •   • g. banana

8. 바나나 •   • h. cup

9. 바구니 •   • i. to be dark

10. 담기다 •   • j. thief

Section II - Comprehension

Look at the picture of someone's room, and fill in the sentences that describe the room with -어 있다.

11. 책 두 권이 책상 위에 _____ .

12. 창문이 _____ .

13. 옷이 의자 위에 _____ .

14. 컵이 바닥에 _____ .

15. 에어컨이 _____ .

Section III - Translation Practice

Complete the translations using -어 있다.

16. When I came to the office in the morning, the window was broken.

 = 제가 아침에 출근했을 때, _____ .

17. The lights are still turned on, so the street is not dark.

 = 아직 _____ 어둡지 않아요.

18. Has the thief been caught in the police station?

 = 그 도둑 경찰서에 _____ ?

19. This town is surrounded by mountains.

 = 이 마을은 _____ .

20. The bananas have been put into the basket.

 = 바나나는 바구니에 _____ .

Section IV - Dictation

Listen to the sentences, and fill in the blanks with the missing word or phrase. The sentences will be played twice.

21. 파란색으로 _____ 간판 _____?

22. 아침에 일어나니까 _____.

Section V - Listening Comprehension

Listen to the dialogue, and answer the following questions. The dialogue will be played twice.

* 파스타 = pasta

23. Choose what you can infer from the dialogue.

    a. 라면집은 점심에 항상 열려 있다.

    b. 여자는 파스타집 문이 닫혀 있는 것을 자주 보았다.

    c. 오늘 점심에는 파스타*집 문이 열려 있을 것이다.

    d. 여자와 남자는 친구 사이다.

24. What can the man not say after lunch?

    a. 오늘 점심 시간에 파스타집 갔는데, 불이 켜져 있었어요.

    b. 오늘은 어제 점심 시간처럼 파스타집 문이 닫혀 있었어요.

    c. 파스타집 문은 닫혀 있고, 라면집 문은 열려 있더라고요.

    d. 파스타집 문이 열려 있길래, 파스타 먹었어요.

Section VI - Speaking Practice

A native speaker will read the dialogue from Section V line by line. Listen and repeat each sentence one by one. You can check out the dialogue in the Answer Key at the end.

Lesson 25.
To be bound to + verb
동사 + -게 되어 있다

Section I - Vocabulary

Use a dictionary to match each Korean word to its common English translation. All words are used in the following sections, so be sure to check out the answer before you move on to the next section and commit them to memory!

1. 꽃 •   • a. body

2. 피다 •   • b. to bloom

3. 봄 •   • c. for sure, at any cost

4. 찌다 •   • d. day, daytime

5. 몸 •   • e. originally, naturally

6. 성공하다 •   • f. to gain (weight)

7. 낮 •   • g. to move

8. 움직이다 •   • h. to succeed

9. 원래 •   • i. spring

10. 꼭 •   • j. flower

Section II - Complete the Dialogue, Part 1

Complete the dialogues by choosing the appropriate expression from each box and conjugating it with -(으)면 -게 되어 있어요.

-(으)면	-게 되어 있어요
많이 먹다	꽃이 피다
봄이 오다	살이 찌다
열심히 하다	건강해지다
운동을 하다	잠이 잘 오다
몸을 많이 쓰다	언젠가 성공하다

11. A: 왜 계속 살이 찌지?

    B: _____ .

12. A: 요즘에 잠이 잘 안 와요.

    B: 낮에 많이 안 움직였죠? _____ .

13. A: 건강해지고 싶어요.

    B: 운동을 하세요. _____ .

14. A: 꽃은 언제 필까요?

    B: 곧 피겠죠. 이제 곧 봄이잖아요. _____ .

15. A: 제가 성공할 수 있을까요?

    B: 그럼요. 현우 씨처럼 _____ .

Section III - Complete the Dialogue, Part 2

Complete the dialogues by choosing the appropriate expression from each box and conjugating it with -(으)면 -게 되어 있더라고요.

-(으)면	-게 되어 있더라고요
일찍 자다	다 좋아하다
공짜라고 하다	잘 치다
몸에서 멀어지다	꼭 실수를 하다
매일 연습하다	일찍 일어나다
서두르다	마음에서도 멀어지다

16. A: 친구가 이사 가니까 연락을 잘 안 하게 됐어요.

    B: 원래 ~~~~~~~~~~~~~~~~~~~~~~~~~~~~~~~~~~~~~ .

17. A: 사람들이 이거 진짜 좋아하더라고요.

    B: 그럼요. 공짜잖아요. ~~~~~~~~~~~~~~~~~~~~~~~ .

18. A: 저도 피아노 잘 치고 싶어요.

    B: 매일 연습해 보세요. 아무리 못 치는 사람도 ~~~~~~~~~ .

19. A: 준배 씨는 어떻게 그렇게 일찍 일어나요?

    B: 일찍 자요. ~~~~~~~~~~~~~~~~~~~~~~~~~~~~~~~ .

20. A: 지금 몇 시예요? 빨리 끝내야 되죠?

    B: 괜찮아요. 천천히 하세요. ~~~~~~~~~~~~~~~~~~ .

Section IV - Dictation

Listen to the sentences, and fill in the blanks with the missing word or phrase. The sentences will be played twice.

21. 그건 ～～～～～～～～～～～～～～～～～～～ .

22. 만나야 할 사람들은 ～～～～～～～～～～～～ .

Section V - Listening Comprehension

23. Listen to the dialogue, and choose the incorrect statement based on the dialogue. The dialogue will be played twice.

   * 늘다 = to improve

   a. The man knows how to become good at speaking.
   b. The man thinks that if someone is good at speaking, they are also good at writing.
   c. The man said that one will be better at speaking if they practice a lot.
   d. The woman thinks that she is good at writing.

Section VI - Speaking Practice

A native speaker will read the dialogue from Section V line by line. Listen and repeat each sentence one by one. You can check out the dialogue in the Answer Key at the end.

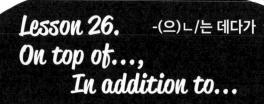

Lesson 26.
On top of...,
In addition to...
-(으)ㄴ/는 데다가

Section I - Vocabulary

Match each Korean word or phrase to its common English translation. All words and phrases are used in the following sections as well, so be sure to commit them to memory!

a. to be kind, to be hospitable	b. to be clean
c. to have a good memory	d. personality, character
e. to be dirty	f. to be good for health
g. to be difficult to make	h. to dance

1. 깨끗하다 ~~~~~~~~~~~~~~~~

2. 더럽다 ~~~~~~~~~~~~~~~~

3. 춤추다 ~~~~~~~~~~~~~~~~

4. 친절하다 ~~~~~~~~~~~~~~~~

5. 성격 ~~~~~~~~~~~~~~~~

6. 기억력이 좋다 ~~~~~~~~~~~~~~~~

7. 만들기 어렵다 ~~~~~~~~~~~~~~~~

8. 건강에 좋다 ~~~~~~~~~~~~~~~~

Section II - Comprehension

Choose the correct word or phrase to complete the
following sentences.

9. 그 집은 _____ 데다가 깨끗해요.

    a. 넓은   b. 더러운   c. 무서운

10. 그 케이크는 예쁜 데다가 _____.

    a. 맛도 없어요   b. 맛도 있어요   c. 맛이 이상해요

11. 그 방은 더러운 데다가 _____.

    a. 맛있어요   b. 싸요   c. 좁아요

12. 이 음식은 맛있는 데다가 _____.

    a. 만들기도 어려워요   b. 건강에 좋아요   c. 가격이 비싸요

13. 그 가수는 _____ 데다가 춤도 잘 춰요.

    a. 노래를 잘하는   b. 노래를 못하는   c. 노래를 싫어하는

Section III - Reading Comprehension

This is a letter from your Korean friend who returned to Korea. Read carefully and answer the questions.

안녕!

얼마 전에 한국에 돌아온 것 같은데, 벌써 1년 됐네.

잘 지내고 있어? 대학 생활*은 어때?

너는 성격도 좋은 데다가 공부도 잘하니까, 아마 잘 하고 있겠지?

2년 전에, 네가 한국 뉴스로 한국어 공부를 해 보고 싶다고 했지?

그래서 이 News in Korean 책을 선물로 보내. 이 책 정말 괜찮더라고.

재미있고 유익한* 데다가, 한국어 시험 준비할 때도 좋아!

이 책으로 잘 공부해 봐! :)

그럼 또 연락할게. 안녕!

소희 씀

* Vocabulary
생활 = life / 유익하다 = to be instructive, to be informative

14. Choose the correct statement according to the letter.

a. Your friend thinks that you have a nice personality, but are not good at studying.

b. Your friend sent you a gift because he/she thought it was a good book.

c. Your friend thinks that studying Korean with news is not a good idea.

d. Your friend thinks that the "News in Korean" book is fun, but not helpful for the exam.

15. If you want to text your friend "In addition to being kind, you also have a good memory", which one is correct?

    a. 너는 친절하은 데다가 기억력도 좋구나.

    b. 너는 친절하는 데다가 기억력도 좋구나.

    c. 너는 친절한 데다가 기억력도 좋구나.

    d. 너는 친절하 데다가 기억력도 좋구나.

Section IV - Dictation

Listen to the sentences, and fill in the blanks with the missing word or phrase. The sentences will be played twice.

16. 이 식당은 _____ 맛도 없어요.

17. 다혜 씨는 _____ 만나기 어려워요.

Section V - Listening Comprehension

18. Listen to the dialogue and choose the <u>incorrect</u> statement. The dialogue will be played twice.

                                            * 골목= alley / * 간판 = signboard

                       * 길치 = directionally challenged / * 홍대= Hongdae; Hongik University area in Seoul

    a. 두 사람이 있는 가게는 좁은 골목에 있고 간판이 없다.

    b. 두 사람이 있는 가게는 찾기 어려운 곳에 있다.

    c. 남자는 여자보다 먼저 도착했다.

    d. 여자는 홍대에 많이 와 본 데다가 길도 잘 안다.

Section VI - Speaking Practice

A native speaker will read the dialogue from Section V line by line. Listen and repeat each sentence one by one. You can check out the dialogue in the Answer Key at the end.

Lesson 27.
As long as
-기만 하면, -(느)ㄴ 한

Section I - Vocabulary

Match each Korean word or phrase to its common English translation. All words and phrases will be used in the following sections as well, so be sure to commit them to memory!

1. 아기 •
2. 엄마 •
3. 결혼 •
4. 허락 •
5. 교수 •
6. 점수 •
7. 과제 •
8. 제출 •
9. 열쇠 •
10. 얼음 •

• a. mom
• b. assignment
• c. mark, grade
• d. submission
• e. baby
• f. professor
• g. marriage
• h. ice
• i. permission, approval
• j. key

Section II - Translation Practice

Complete the sentences using -기만 하면, -(느)ㄴ 한, -지만 않으면, or -지 않는 한.

11. _____, 한국어 잘할 수 있어요.

    = As long as you study Korean in a fun way, you can become good at Korean.

12. _____, 아무도 못 들어가요.

    = As long as I have the keys, no one can go in.

13. _____, 갈게요.

    = As long as it is not too hot, I will go/come.

14. _____, 계속 쓸 수 있어요.

    = As long as it is not broken, you can keep using it.

15. _____, 괜찮아요.

    = As long as not too many people come here, it is okay.

Section III - Comprehension

Rewrite what B says using the given structure.

16. -지만 않으면

    A: 우리 내일 한강 가요?

    B: 네. 비만 안 오면 갈 거예요.

    ↪ _____
    _____

17. -기만 하면

    A: 아기가 안 우네요.

    B: 네. 엄마랑 같이 있으면 안 울어요.

    ➜ ～～～～～～～～～～～～～～～～～～～～～～～～～～～

18. -(느)ㄴ 한

    A: 어머니, 저희 결혼을 허락해 주세요!

    B: 내가 살아 있는 동안에는 절대 허락할 수 없다.

    ➜ ～～～～～～～～～～～～～～～～～～～～～～～～～～～

19. -지 않는 한

    A: 물이 많이 차가운데, 괜찮겠어요?

    B: 얼음물처럼 차갑지만 않으면 괜찮아요. 주세요.

    ➜ ～～～～～～～～～～～～～～～～～～～～～～～～～～～

20. -기만 하면

    A: 이번 과제 너무 어려워요.

    B: 그래서 교수님이 시간 안에 제출만 하면 좋은 점수 주신다고 하셨어요.

    ➜ ～～～～～～～～～～～～～～～～～～～～～～～～～～～

Section IV - Dictation

Listen to the sentences, and fill in the blanks with the missing word or phrase.
The sentences will be played twice.

21. ～～～～～～～～～～～ 이번 주 수요일에 수영장에 갈 거예요.

22. ～～～～～～～～～～～～～～～ 문제 없을 거예요.

Section V - Listening Comprehension

23. Listen to the dialogue, and choose which statements are correct and which are incorrect. The dialogue will be played twice.

    a. 남자는 소파에서도 잘 잘 수 있다.

    b. 여자는 남자가 추워서 못 잘 것 같다고 걱정하고 있다.

    c. 여자는 남자한테 창문을 열고 자라고 말했다.

    d. 남자는 추운 곳에서도 잘 잔다.

    • Correct statements: ~~~~~~~~~~~~~~~~~

    • Incorrect statements: ~~~~~~~~~~~~~~~~~

Section VI - Speaking Practice

A native speaker will read the dialogue from Section V line by line. Listen and repeat each sentence one by one. You can check out the dialogue in the Answer Key at the end.

Lesson 28.
The thing that is called + verb
-(ㄴ/는)다는 것

Section I - Vocabulary

Match each Korean word or phrase to its common English translation. All words and phrases will be used in the following sections as well, so be sure to commit them to memory!

1. 쉽지 않다 •

2. 혼자 보내다 •

3. 휴가를 쓰다 •

4. 외롭다 •

5. 혼자 공부하다 •

6. 직업으로 갖다 •

7. 시험을 보다 •

8. 대단하다 •

9. 무모하다 •

10. 스트레스받다 •

• a. to take an exam

• b. to get stressed

• c. to have it as a job

• d. to be lonely

• e. to take days off

• f. to be reckless

• g. to be amazing

• h. to spend by oneself

• i. to be not easy

• j. to study by oneself

Section II - Complete the Sentence

-(ㄴ/는)다는 것은 -(으)ㄴ/는 일이에요 is a commonly used structure. Complete the sentences using the word or phrase in Section I.

11. 일요일을 〰〰〰〰〰〰〰〰〰〰〰〰〰〰〰〰〰〰〰〰〰〰〰〰.

    = Spending Sunday by yourself is a lonely thing.

12. 싫어하는 일을 〰〰〰〰〰〰〰〰〰〰〰〰〰〰〰〰〰〰〰.

    = Having something you don't like to do as a job is a stressful thing.

13. 선생님 없이 〰〰〰〰〰〰〰〰〰〰〰〰〰〰〰〰〰〰〰〰.

    = Studying by yourself without a teacher is not an easy thing.

14. 공부를 전혀 하지 않고 〰〰〰〰〰〰〰〰〰〰〰〰〰〰〰.

    = Taking an exam without studying at all is a reckless thing.

15. 그 사람을 위해 〰〰〰〰〰〰〰〰〰〰〰〰〰〰〰〰〰〰.

    = Taking days off for that person is an amazing thing.

Section III - Translation Practice

The following sentences are from Level 7 Lesson 28.
Fill in the blanks using -(ㄴ/는)다는 것.

16. 〰〰〰〰〰〰〰〰〰〰〰〰〰〰 은 언제나 즐거운 일이에요.

    = Learning is always a pleasant thing to do.

17. 〰〰〰〰〰〰〰〰〰〰〰〰〰〰 은 가끔 힘들 때도 있어요.

    = The nature of living overseas is that there are sometimes hard times.

18. 〰〰〰〰〰〰〰〰〰〰〰〰〰〰 은 참 힘든 일이에요.

    = Raising a child is very tough.

19. _____ 은 정말 어려운 일이에요.

= Becoming a famous singer in Korea is a very difficult thing.

20. _____ 은 정말 대단한 일이에요.

= Receiving a scholarship is (an) amazing (achievement).

Section IV - Dictation

Listen to the sentences, and fill in the blanks with the missing word or phrase. The sentences will be played twice.

21. 주말에도 _____ 정말 슬픈 일이에요.

22. _____ 아름다운 일이에요.

Section V - Listening Comprehension

23. Listen to the dialogue, and choose the correct statement based on the dialogue. The dialogue will be played twice.

* 내용 = content, story

a. The man had already seen the movie that the woman recommended.

b. The movie that the woman recommended is about what it is to become a father.

c. The woman asked the movie director about the movie's story.

d. The movie that the woman recommended is about what it is to become a family.

Section VI - Speaking Practice

A native speaker will read the dialogue from Section V line by line. Listen and repeat each sentence one by one. You can check out the dialogue in the Answer Key at the end.

Lesson 29.
So that...,
To the point where...

-도록

Section I - Vocabulary

Match each Korean word or phrase to its common English translation. Be sure to check out the answer before you move on to the next section and commit them to memory!

1. 길을 막다 •   • a. to feel bloated (lit. stomach bursts)

2. 배가 터지다 •   • b. to listen to a song

3. 수업을 듣다 •   • c. to be heard, can hear

4. 노래를 듣다 •   • d. to throw away/out garbage

5. 쓰레기를 버리다 •   • e. to block the way

6. 들리다 •   • f. to fall over, to fall down

7. 보이다 •   • g. to take classes

8. 질리다 •   • h. to be seen, can see

9. 떨어지다 •   • i. to get sick of

10. 넘어지다 •   • j. to wear out

Section II - Translation Practice

Fill in the blanks using -도록.

11. _____ 서둘러 주세요.

= Please hurry up so that you won't be late.

12. _____ 주의해 주세요.

= Please be careful so that you don't fall over.

13. _____ 크게 써 주세요.

= Please write it big so that (everyone) even in the back can see it.

14. _____ 천천히 말해 주세요.

= Please speak slowly so that I can understand.

15. _____ 크게 말해 주세요.

= Please speak loud so that the people in the back can also hear it.

Section III - Complete the Dialogue

Fill in the blanks using -도록.

16. A: 밥 많이 먹었어요?

B: 네. _____ .

A: Have you eaten a lot?

B: Yes. I ate to the point where I felt bloated.

17. A: 제가 추천한 노래 들어 봤어요?

B: 네, _____ .

A: Have you listened to the song that I recommended?

B: Yes, the song was so good that I listened to it to the point where I got sick of it.

18. A: 죄송한데, ～～～～～～～～～～～～～ 조금만 비켜 주시겠어요?

   B: 앗, 죄송해요. 제가 길을 막고 있는 줄 몰랐어요.

   A: Excuse me, but could you please step aside just a little bit so that people can pass through?

   B: Oops, I'm sorry. I didn't know I was blocking the way.

19. A: 제가 종이 쓰레기는 일요일에 버려야 한다고 ～～～～～～～～～～～～

   얘기했는데, 왜 오늘 버렸어요?

   B: 앗, 죄송해요. 또 잊었어요.

   A: I told you (so many times) that you have to throw out paper waste on Sundays to the point that my mouth hurts. Why did you throw it out today?

   B: Oops, I'm sorry. I forgot again.

20. A: 한국어 공부를 하려고 하는데, 어떤 선생님 수업을 듣는 게 좋을까요?

   B: 선현우 선생님 수업 추천해요. ～～～～～～～～～ 잘 설명해 주시거든요.

   A: I'm planning to study the Korean language. Which teacher do you think I should take classes from?

   B: I recommend teacher Hyunwoo Sun's class because he explains things well so that students find it easy to understand.

Section IV - Dictation

Listen to the sentences, and fill in the blanks with the missing word or phrase. The sentences will be played twice.

21. 이 신발은 ～～～～～～～～～～～～ 자주 신었어요.

22. 요즘 ～～～～～～～～～～～～ 잠을 잘 못 잤어요.

Section V - Listening Comprehension

23. Listen to the dialogue, and choose the <u>incorrect</u> statement based on the dialogue. The dialogue will be played twice.

a. 여자는 밤늦게까지 잠을 못 잤다.

b. 여자는 밤에도 일을 했다.

c. 남자는 주말에 질릴 만큼 잠을 잘 것이다.

d. 오늘은 금요일이다.

Section VI - Speaking Practice

A native speaker will read the dialogue from Section V line by line. Listen and repeat each sentence one by one. You can check out the dialogue in the Answer Key at the end.

Section I - Vocabulary

Use a dictionary to match each Korean word to its common English translation. All words are used in the following sections, so be sure to check out the answer before you move on to the next section and commit them to memory!

a. to agree with what one says

b. to be friends with

c. to be a good conversation partner, to connect well

d. to give up in the middle

e. atmosphere is nice

f. to have similar personalities, to get along well together

g. to confess one's feelings

h. computer is slow

i. to meet with good results, to come to good

j. to upload consistently

1. 말에 동의하다 ﹏﹏﹏

2. 컴퓨터가 느리다 ﹏﹏﹏

3. 좋은 결과를 얻다 ﹏﹏﹏

4. 분위기가 좋다 ﹏﹏﹏

5. 꾸준히 올리다 ﹏﹏﹏

6. 중간에 포기하다 ﹏﹏﹏

7. 대화가 잘 통하다 ﹏﹏﹏

8. 성격이 잘 맞다 ﹏﹏﹏

9. 마음을 고백하다 ﹏﹏﹏

10. 친구로 지내다 ﹏﹏﹏

Section II - Matching

Take a sentence fragment from column A, match it with the most appropriate fragment from column B, and write it as one sentence on the line below.

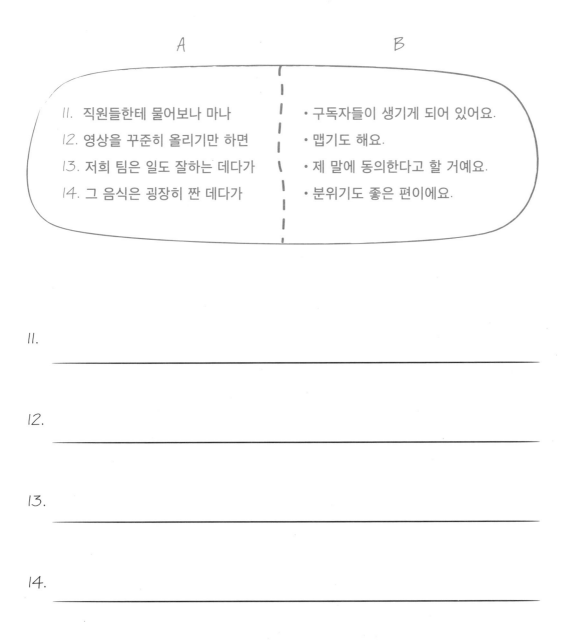

A

B

11. 직원들한테 물어보나 마나

12. 영상을 꾸준히 올리기만 하면

13. 저희 팀은 일도 잘하는 데다가

14. 그 음식은 굉장히 짠 데다가

• 구독자들이 생기게 되어 있어요.

• 맵기도 해요.

• 제 말에 동의한다고 할 거예요.

• 분위기도 좋은 편이에요.

11.

12.

13.

14.

	A	B
15.	밥을 주나 마나	• 또 배고프다고 할 거예요.
16.	덜 먹고 열심히 운동하기만 하면	• 소리도 크게 나는 편이에요.
17.	중간에 공부를 포기하지만 않으면	• 살이 빠지게 되어 있어요.
18.	그 컴퓨터는 너무 느린 데다가	• 좋은 결과를 얻게 되어 있어요.

15. _____

16. _____

17. _____

18. _____

Section III - Reading Comprehension

This is a letter sent into a radio show. Read it carefully and answer the questions.

안녕하세요! 저는 한국에 사는 대학생 지나라고 합니다.

저는 제 친구 석진이를 5년 동안 좋아하고 있어요. 저희는 고등학생 때부터 친구였어요. 석진이는 잘생긴 데다가 키가 큰 편이에요. 그리고 성격도 저랑 잘맞고, 대화도 잘 통해요. 그래서 석진이를 좋아하게 됐어요.

제 친구들은 제가 석진이한테 제 마음을 고백했으면 좋겠다고 해요. 하지만 고백하나 마나 잘 안 될 것 같아요. 석진이는 저를 좋아하지 않는 것 같아요. 고백하지만 않으면 저와 석진이는 계속 친구로 지낼 수 있을 거예요. 그런데 고백을 하면 친구로 못 지낼 수도 있잖아요. 그게 걱정이에요. 그래도 고백해 보는 게 더 좋을까요? 제 이야기를 읽어 주셔서 감사합니다.

19. Choose the incorrect statement according to the letter.

   a. 지나는 석진이한테 고백을 해 봤자 소용없을 거라고 생각한다.

   b. 지나는 석진이한테 고백을 하지 않는 것이 더 좋을 수도 있다고 생각한다.

   c. 지나는 석진이가 키가 큰 데다가 공부도 잘해서 석진이를 좋아한다.

   d. 지나의 친구들은 지나가 석진이를 좋아하는 것을 알고 있다.

20. Rewrite the underlined sentence using -(으)ㄴ/는 데다가 -(으)ㄴ/는 편이에요.

   성격도 저랑 잘 맞고, 대화도 잘 통해요.

   = _____ .

Section IV - Dictation

Listen to the sentences, and fill in the blanks with the missing word or phrase. The sentences will be played twice.

21. ~~_____~~ 바쁘다고 할 거예요.

22. 여기는 날씨도 ~~_____~~ 이에요.

Section V - Listening Comprehension

23. Listen to the dialogue, and choose the correct statement according to the dialogue. The dialogue will be played twice.

* 비행기가 결항되다 = the flight is canceled

a. 남자는 내일 아침 비행기가 분명히 결항될 것이라고 생각한다.

b. 비가 많이 오지 않는 한, 비행기는 결항되지 않는다.

c. 비 오는 날보다 바람 부는 날에 비행기가 결항되는 일이 더 많다.

d. 내일은 날씨가 좋을 것이다.

Section VI - Speaking Practice

A native speaker will read the dialogue from Section V line by line. Listen and repeat one by one. You can check out the dialogue in the Answer Key at the end.

Answer Key
for
TTMIK
Workbook
Level 7

Lesson 1

Section I - Vocabulary

1. a   2. h   3. g   4. c   5. f

6. j   7. b   8. e   9. i   10. d

Section II - Translation Practice

11. 물이 정말 차갑군요

12. 한국 날씨가 얼마나 추운지 몰랐구나

13. 여기 진짜 넓구나/크구나

14. 한국어(를) 정말 잘하(시)는군요

15. 다혜 씨가 아직 대학생이(시)군요 or 다혜 씨는 아직 대학생이(시)군요

Section III - Fill in the Blank

16. (너) 정말 게으르구나 / 이번 달에 바빴구나

17. 정말 뜨겁군요 / 못 참는구나 / 그렇구나

Section IV - Reading Comprehension

<Translation>

My Korean friends often say "그렇구나 (= I see)" when they talk. Koreans always say "아~ 진짜? (= Oh, really?)" or "아~ 그렇구나! (= Oh, I see!)" after they listen to others. A lot of Koreans say those phrases. And Korean people also use "그랬구나! (= I see!)" a lot. If I tell my friend that it was a hard day today, they say "그랬구나 (= I see)" and console me. I am thankful that my friends always listen to me carefully.

18. b

Section V - Dictation

19. 어제도 만났군요.

(= (I didn't know before, but I just found out that) You met yesterday too.)

20. 아들: 엄마, 이거 드셔 보세요. 제가 만들었어요.

(= Son: Mom, please try some. I made it.)

엄마: 와, 정말 맛있다! 우리 아들이 요리를 정말 잘하는구나.

(= Mom: Wow, it's so good! (I didn't know before, but I just found out that) my son is a good cook.)

Section VI - Listening Comprehension

<Transcript>

남자: 이 신발 누구 거예요? 진짜 귀엽다.

여자: 주연이 신발이에요.

남자: 와! 주연이 발이 진짜 작군요.

여자: 네. 주연이가 키에 비해서 발이 작은 편이에요.

남자: 아, 그렇군요.

Man: Whose shoes are these? They are so cute.

Woman: They are Jooyeon's shoes.

Man: Wow! (I didn't know before, but I just realized that) Jooyeon's feet are very small!

Woman: Yes. Jooyeon's feet are relatively small compared to her height.

Man: Oh, I see.

21. a   22. b

Section VII - Speaking Practice

남자: 이 신발 누구 거예요?

[이 신발 누구 꺼예요?]

진짜 귀엽다.

[진짜 귀엽따.]

여자: 주연이 신발이에요.

[주여니 신바리에요.]

남자: 와! 주연이 발이 진짜 작군요.

[와! 주여니 바리 진짜 작꾼뇨.]

여자: 네. 주연이가 키에 비해서 발이 작은 편이에요.

[네. 주여니가 키에 비해서 바리 자근 펴니에요.]

남자: 아, 그렇군요.

[아, 그러쿤뇨.]

Lesson 2

Section I - Vocabulary

1. g   2. a   3. c   4. f   5. d

6. e   7. b   8. h   9. j   10. i

Section II - Comprehension

11. a   12. b   13. b   14. d   15. b

Section III - Translation Practice

16. 귀여운 척

17. 말이 없는 척하고 있 or 말이 없는 체하고 있, 말이 많아요

18. 바쁜 척했어요 or 바쁜 체했어요

19. 아는 척했어요 or 아는 체했어요

20. 자는 척할/체할 거예요 or 자고 있는 척/체할 거예요

Section IV - Dictation

21. 어젯밤에 공부한 척하지 마세요. 파티에 갔잖아요!

    (= Don't pretend that you studied last night. You went to the party, didn't you!)

22. 다른 사람들한테는 비밀이에요. 모르는 척해 주세요.

    (= It's a secret to everyone else. Please pretend you don't know it.)

23. 그 사람은 예쁜 척을 너무 많이 해요.

    (= She behaves (too much) like she's pretty.)

Section V - Listening Comprehension

<Transcript>

여자: 아까 왜 저 못 본 척했어요?

남자: 언제요?

여자: 아까 복도에서 제가 인사했는데 못 본 척했잖아요.

남자: 아, 정말요? 아니에요. 진짜 못 봤어요. 죄송해요.

Woman: Why did you pretend not to see me earlier?

Man: When?

Woman: A little while ago in the hall. I said hello, and you pretended you didn't see me, didn't you?

Man: Oh, really? No way. I really didn't see you. I'm sorry.

24. b   25. a

Section VI - Speaking Practice

여자: 아까 왜 저 못 본 척했어요?

[아까 왜 저 몯 뽄 처캐써요?]

남자: 언제요?

[언제요?]

여자: 아까 복도에서 제가 인사했는데 못 본 척했잖아요.

[아까 복또에서 제가 인사핸는데 몯 뽄 처캗짜나요.]

남자: 아, 정말요?

[아, 정마료*?]

아니에요.

[아니에요.]

진짜 못 봤어요.

[진짜 몯 빠써요.]

죄송해요.

[죄송해요.]

* Native speakers often pronounce 정말요 as [정말료] as well.

Lesson 3

Section I - Vocabulary

1. g   2. c   3. a   4. b   5. h

6. e   7. j   8. i   9. f   10. d

Section II - Comprehension

11. b   12. c   13. b

14. b   15. c   16. a

Section III - Reading Comprehension

<Translation>

I went to Sohee's home today. Sohee's mom cooked 불고기 and 된장찌개 for us. It was really delicious, so I told Sohee's mom, "먹을 만하네요." Then, Sohee said, "Haha, it's not polite to say something like that in front of the person who cooked the food. It's better to just say "맛있어요. (= It's delicious.)" I was so surprised, and told Sohee's mom again. "Sorry. So what I meant was, it's really delicious!" I'm glad I learned a new thing because of the mistake though.

17. b   18. c   19. a

Section IV - Dictation

20. 경주에 가 보셨어요? 한국 역사를 좋아하시면 가 볼 만해요.

(= Have you ever been to Gyeongju? If you like Korean history, it's worth a visit.)

21. 어제 일을 많이 해서 머리가 좀 아파요. 그래도 괜찮 아요. 참을 만해요.

(= I worked a lot yesterday, so I have a little head-ache. It's okay, though. I can bear it.)

Section V - Listening Comprehension

<Transcript>

남자: 요즘 볼 만한 드라마 없어요?

여자: 비밀의 숲이라는 드라마 알아요?

남자: 아니요. 그 드라마 재밌어요?

여자: 네, 진짜 재밌어요. 꼭 보세요. 정말 볼 만해요.

Man: Are there any good dramas these days?

Woman: Do you know the drama called Stranger (Literal title: "Secret Forest")?

Man: No. Is it good?

Woman: Yes, it's really good. You should definitely watch it. It's really worth watching.

22. c   23. c

Section VI - Speaking Practice

남자: 요즘 볼 만한 드라마 없어요?

[요즘 볼 만한 드라마 업써요?]

여자: 비밀의 숲이라는 드라마 알아요?

[비미레 수피라는 드라마 아라요?]

남자: 아니요.

[아니요.]

그 드라마 재밌어요?

[그 드라마 재미써요?]

여자: 네, 진짜 재밌어요.

[네, 진짜 재미써요.]

꼭 보세요.

[꼭 보세요.]

정말 볼 만해요.

[정말 볼 만해요.]

Lesson 4

Section I - Vocabulary

1. e   2. b   3. d   4. c   5. h
6. f   7. g   8. i   9. a

Section II - Comprehension

10. incorrect - 같이/처럼	11. incorrect - 같은
12. correct	13. incorrect - 같이/처럼
14. correct	15. correct
16. correct	

Section III - Reading Comprehension

<Translation>

I think Korean people like "to do things together", especially to eat something together. I also like to eat together with my friends. When I have a meal with my friends, I feel like they are my family. My Korean friends also go to the restroom together and wait for each other. At first, I felt awkward going to the restroom together with my friends, but now, like my Korean friends, I also come along when they go to the restroom. Like Korean people, I also came to like "to do things together".

17. b   18. d

Section IV - Dictation

19. 제 친구는 <u>미국 사람인데 한국 사람같이 한국어를 잘</u> 해요.

    (= My friend is an American, but he/she is good at Korean like Korean people.)

20. 저는 새들처럼 하늘을 날고 싶어요.

    (= I want to fly in the sky like birds.)

Section V - Listening Comprehension

\<Transcript>

남자: 둘이 항상 같이 다녀요?

여자: 네. 저희는 가족 같은 사이예요.

남자: 둘이 나이 차이 많이 나지 않아요?

여자: 많이 나는데 저희는 친구처럼 지내요.

Man: Are you two always together?

Woman: Yes. We are like family.

Man: Isn't there a big age gap between you two?

Woman: There is, but we get along with each other like friends.

21. d   22. c

Section VI - Speaking Practice

남자: 둘이 항상 같이 다녀요?

    [두리 항상 가치 다녀요?]

여자: 네. 저희는 가족 같은 사이예요.

    [네. 저히는 가족 가튼 사이예요.]

남자: 둘이 나이 차이 많이 나지 않아요?

    [두리 나이 차이 마:니 나지 아나요?]

여자: 많이 나는데 저희는 친구처럼 지내요.

    [마:니 나는데 저히는 친구처럼 지내요.]

Lesson 5

Section I - Vocabulary

1. f   2. c   3. b   4. d   5. a

6. e   7. i   8. g   9. h   10. j

Section II - Complete the Dialogue

11. 제 손만큼

12. 원하는 만큼 가져오세요

13. 이만큼

14. 일한 만큼

15. 놀랄 만큼

Section III - Reading Comprehension

\<Translation>

In Korea, there are a lot of all-you-can-eat restaurants. At all-you-can-eat restaurants, you can eat as much food as you want to eat. However, this is always written: "Take just the amount that you will eat.", "Take just the amount that you need." A lot of people take a lot of food, but they cannot eat it all and have some left over. All the leftover food is thrown away as trash. Therefore, to protect the environment, you have to take just the amount of food that you will eat.

16. c   17. c

Section IV - Dictation

18. 여기 오렌지 많이 있으니까, <u>먹고 싶은 만큼 가져가세요.</u>

    (= There are a lot of oranges here, so take as many as you want to eat.)

19. A: 여기요, 휴지 좀 주세요.

(= Excuse me, can you get me some tissues?)

B: 네, 얼마만큼 드려요?

(= Okay, how many do you want?)

20. 너 밥 그만큼만 먹을 거야?

(= Are you going to eat just that much rice?)

Section V - Listening Comprehension

<Transcript>

남자: 시험 잘 봤어요?

여자: 공부한 만큼은 못 본 것 같아요. 문제가 너무 어려웠어요.

남자: 그래서 아무것도 못 썼어요?

여자: 그냥 아는 만큼 썼어요.

Man: Did you do well on your exam?

Woman: I don't think I did as well as I studied. The questions were too difficult.

Man: So you couldn't write anything?

Woman: I just wrote as much as I know.

21. c   22. a

Section VI - Speaking Practice

남자: 시험 잘 봤어요?

[시험 잘 봐써요?]

여자: 공부한 만큼은 못 본 것 같아요.

[공부한 만크믄 몯 뽄 걷 가타요.]

문제가 너무 어려웠어요.

[문제가 너무 어려워써요.]

남자: 그래서 아무것도 못 썼어요?

[그래서 아무걷또 몯 써써요?]

여자: 그냥 아는 만큼 썼어요.

[그냥 아는 만큼 써써요.]

Lesson 6

Section I - Vocabulary

1. 병원(病院): hospital

2. 퇴원(退院): leaving the hospital, being discharged from the hospital

3. 대학원(大學院): graduate school

4. 원장(院長): head of an organization or an institute whose name ends with -원

5. 연구원(研究院): research center

6. 입원(入院): being hospitalized, hospitalization

7. 학원(學院): private school, institute

8. 한의원(韓醫院): oriental medicine clinic

Section II - Fill in the Blank

I'm working at a private school in Korea.

My head teacher is a good person.

9. 학원   10. 원장

My friend is sick, so he/she has been hospitalized.

He/she said that he/she will be discharged from the hospital in three days.

11. 병원   12. 입원   13. 퇴원

My father is a scientist, so he works at a research center.

My mother is an oriental medical doctor, so she works at an oriental medicine clinic.

I also want to become a professor in the future after studying hard at a graduate school.

14. 연구원   15. 한의원   16. 대학원

Section III - Comprehension

17. b (원 as in 공원 is based on 園, which means "garden".)

18. c (원 as in 만 원 is a native Korean word, which is the unit of money used in Korea.)

19. b (원 as in 회사원 is based on 員, which means "member".)

20. c (원 as in 원하다 is based on 願, which means "to want".)

21. b (원 as in 직원 is based on 員, which means "member".)

Section IV - Dictation

22. 저는 대학을 졸업하고 대학원에 갈 거예요.

(= I'm going to graduate school after graduating from university.)

23. 원장 선생님이 그렇게 말씀하셨어요.

(= My head teacher told me so.)

Section V - Listening Comprehension

\<Transcript\>

여자: 무슨 일 하세요?

남자: 학원을 운영하고 있어요.

여자: 아! 학원 원장님이시군요.

남자: 네. 맞아요.

Woman: What do you do?

Man: I am running a private school.

Woman: Oh! You are the head of a private school!

Man: Yes. That's right.

24. b

Section VI - Speaking Practice

여자: 무슨 일 하세요?

[무슨 닐 하세요?]

남자: 학원을 운영하고 있어요.

[하궈늘 우녕하고 이써요.]

여자: 아! 학원 원장님이시군요.

[아! 하권 원장니미시군뇨.]

남자: 네. 맞아요.

[네. 마자요.]

Lesson 7

Section I - Vocabulary

1. g	2. h	3. i	4. d	5. j
6. e	7. a	8. c	9. b	10. f

Section II - Translation Practice

11. 전화해 봤자   12. 집에 있어 봤자

13. 우는 척해 봤자   14. 지금 후회해 봤자

15. 일찍 가 봤자

Section III - Comprehension

16. c

Sohee: I'm hungry.

Jina: There's bread here. Do you want some?

Sohee: No, I'm fine. The bread is too small, so I don't think I'll be full even if I eat it.

17. a

Sohee: Soccer is too difficult.

Jina: Have you practiced hard?

Sohee: Yes, but I still can't do it well even if I try hard.

18. c

Sohee: Dahye said she doesn't want to come with us.

Jina: Shall I try talking to her?

Sohee: It won't work even if you do.

19. c

Sohee: Did something happen yesterday?

Jina: Sorry? I don't know anything.

Sohee: Even if you pretend you don't know, it won't work.

20. b

Sohee: This cake tastes really good.

Jina: You're right. It's really good. Is this cake expensive?

Sohee: I don't really know. However, <u>even if it's expensive, it will still only be around 30,000 won.</u>

Section IV - Dictation

21. 제가 말해 봤자 소용없을 거예요. 제 말은 안 들어요.

(= Even if I talk to them, it will not help. They don't listen to me.)

22. <u>지금 가 봤자예요.</u> 비행기가 30분 후에 출발할 거예요.

(= There is no use in going there now. The plane will depart in 30 minutes.)

Section V - Listening Comprehension

<Transcript>

여자: 어? 오빠, 안녕하세요. 주말인데 왜 학교 왔어요?

남자: 집에 있어 봤자 할 일도 없어서 왔어.

여자: 언제까지 있을 거예요?

남자: 저녁까지 있으려고. 일찍 가 봤자 아무도 없어.

Woman: Huh? Hi Kyung-seok! Why did you come to school on the weekend?

Man: There's nothing to do even if I am home, so I came.

Woman: Until when will you be here?

Man: I am going to stay here until the evening. Even if I go home early, there is no one (there).

23. b   24. c

Section VI - Speaking Practice

여자: 어? 오빠, 안녕하세요.

[어? 오빠, 안녕하세요.]

주말인데 왜 학교 왔어요?

[주마린데 왜 학꾜 와써요?]

남자: 집에 있어 봤자 할 일도 없어서 왔어.

[지베 이써 봗짜 할릴도 업써서 와써.]

여자: 언제까지 있을 거예요?

[언제까지 이쓸 꺼예요?]

남자: 저녁까지 있으려고. 일찍 가 봤자 아무도 없어.

[저녁까지 이쓰려고. 일찍 가 봗짜 아무도 업써.]

Lesson 8

Section I - Vocabulary

1. e	2. g	3. d	4. j	5. b
6. c	7. f	8. i	9. a	10. h

Section II - Translation Practice

11. 비가 오길래

12. 책이 5,000원이길래 or 책이 오천 원이길래

13. 뭐라고 (말)했길래

14. 끝날 것 같길래

15. 너무 피곤하길래

Section III - Comprehension

16. b

Yeji: Where were you to make you unable to pick up the phone?

Seung-wan: Oh, I was at the library.

17. c

Yeji: Why did you bring your umbrella? It's not raining.

Seung-wan: It seemed like it would rain, so I brought it. However, it's not raining.

18. a

Dahye: Have you been in the new teacher's class? Isn't he/she so funny?

Dong-geun: I wonder how funny he/she is because everyone talks about him/her?

19. a

Yeji: Why didn't you bring a chair?

Seung-wan: Hyunwoo said he would bring one, so I didn't bring one.

20. b

Yeji: Wow, there are so many people!

Seung-wan: How many are there to make you say so?

Section IV - Reading Comprehension

<Translation>

TTMIK NEWS

Headlines:

Article 1> The Famous Drama OOOO, Four Out of Ten Koreans Saw It... How Interesting is It (to Be Popular Like That)?

Article 2> "Koreans are Good at Playing Online Games, So..." Students from Other Countries who Came to Korea to Learn How to Play Games

Article 3> Singer OO, Revealed His/Her Selfie... "My Fans Said They Wanted to See It, So..."

Article 4> Palme d'Or, What the Korean Movie "XXX" Received... What Prize is It (to Make People Talk about It)?

21. a   22. c   23. a   24. a   25. b   26. c

Section V - Dictation

27. <u>누구를 만나길래 그렇게 예쁜 옷을 입었어요?</u>

(= Who are you meeting to be wearing pretty clothes like that?)

28. <u>뭘 먹었길래 배가 아파요?</u>

(= What did you eat to have a stomach ache?)

Section VI - Listening Comprehension

<Transcript>

여자: 여러분, 떡볶이 드세요.

남자: 우와! 맛있겠다.

여자: 망원 시장에서 이 떡볶이를 먹어 봤는데 너무 맛있길래 사 왔어요.

남자: 그렇지 않아도 이 집 떡볶이가 엄청 유명하길래 먹어 보고 싶었는데! 잘 먹겠습니다.

Woman: Everyone, have some tteokbokki.

Man: Wow! It looks yummy!

Woman: I tried this tteokbokki at Mangwon Market, and it was really good, so I bought it.

Man: Actually, I also wanted to try this tteokbokki because it is really famous! Thank you for the treat.

29. c   30. b

Section VII - Speaking Practice

여자: 여러분, 떡볶이 드세요.

[여러분, 떡뽀끼 드세요.]

남자: 우와! 맛있겠다.

[우와! 마싣껟따.]

여자: 망원 시장에서 이 떡볶이를 먹어 봤는데 너무 맛있길래 사 왔어요.

[망원 시장에서 이 떡뽀끼를 머거 봔는데 너무 마싣낄래 사 와써요.]

남자: 그렇지 않아도 이 집 떡볶이가 엄청 유명하길래 먹어 보고 싶었는데!

[그러치 아나도 이 집 떡뽀끼가 엄청 유명하길래 머거 보고 시펃는데!]

잘 먹겠습니다.

[잘 먹껟씀니다.]

Lesson 9

Section I - Vocabulary

1. i	2. b	3. e	4. a	5. j
6. g	7. f	8. h	9. d	10. c

Section II - Translation Practice

11. 공부하느라고 바빴어요

12. 준비하느라고 못 들었어요

13. 운동하느라고 전화를 못 받을 거예요

14. 먹느라고 돈을 다 썼어요

15. 먹을 것을 찾느라고 잠깐 냉장고를 열었어요

Section III - Complete the Dialogue

16. c

Hyunwoo: Were you not busy today?

Kyeong-eun: Yes, I was hectic cooking because I had a guest.

17. a

Hyunwoo: What were you doing to be so late?

Kyeong-eun: I'm sorry. I was late because I was buying a gift.

18. a

Hyunwoo: Do you want to meet at three o'clock?

Kyeong-eun: I probably won't be able to because I have a meeting. How about at four o'clock?

19. c

Hyunwoo: You've had a really hard time studying, right? Congratulations on finishing it.

Kyeong-eun: It was tough, but I had fun!

20. a

Dahye: Why did you not pick up the phone?

Dong-geun: Oh, I was taking a shower. Why did you call?

Section IV - Comprehension

21. O

22. X (The subject of the two verbs should be the same when you use -느라고.)

23. X (The subject of the two verbs should be the same when you use -느라고.)

24. O

25. O

26. X (You cannot make an imperative or a "let's" sentence using -느라고.)

Section V - Dictation

27. 이번 한 주 동안 시험 준비 하느라고 바빴어요.

   (= I was busy preparing for an exam this week.)

28. 운전하느라고 핸드폰을 못 봤어요.

   (= I was driving, so I couldn't see my phone.)

Section VI - Listening Comprehension

<Transcript>

남자: 여보세요.

여자: 계속 전화했는데, 뭐 하느라고 전화 못 받았어요?

남자: 죄송해요. 청소하느라고 진동 소리를 못 들었어요. 무슨 일이에요?

Man: Hello.

Woman: I kept calling you. What were you doing to not answer my calls?

Man: I am sorry. I was vacuuming, so I couldn't hear the phone vibrating. What's up?

29. c   30. b

Section VII - Speaking Practice

남자: 여보세요.

   [여보세요.]

여자: 계속 전화했는데, 뭐 하느라고 전화 못 받았어요?

[계속 전화핻는데, 뭐 하느라고 전화 몯빠써요?]

남자: 죄송해요.

[죄송해요.]

청소하느라고 진동 소리를 못 들었어요.

[청소하느라고 진동 소리를 몯뜨러써요.]

무슨 일이에요?

[무슨니리에요?]

Lesson 10

Section I - Vocabulary

1. b	2. a	3. j	4. e	5. h
6. i	7. c	8. d	9. f	10. g

Section II - Matching

11. 과장님은 지금 회의하느라고 바쁘신데, 무슨 일이세요?

(= My manager is busy having a meeting right now. What can I help you with?)

12. 그 친구를 만나느라고 저랑 못 만났군요.

(= I see that you couldn't meet me because you were meeting that friend.)

13. 아무리 걱정해 봤자 해결되는 건 없어요.

(= No matter how much you worry, nothing is solved.)

14. 사무실이 조용하길래 아무도 없는 줄 알았어요.

(= Since the office was quiet, I thought nobody was there.)

15. 예쁜 걸 그룹 가수처럼 저도 예쁜 척해 봤어요.

(= I tried pretending to be pretty like a pretty girl group member.)

Section III - Comprehension

16. 저녁에 비가 올 것 같길래

17. 하루 종일 무거운 우산을 들고 다니느라고

18. 우산을 써 봤자

19. 집에 우유가 없길래

20. 우유가 있었구나

21. 출근 준비를 하느라고

22. 사무실에 아무도 없길래

23. 영화배우처럼 멋있는 척하고 있었어요

24. 안 부끄러운 척했어요

Section IV - Dictation

25. 그 사람이 계속 전화하길래 그냥 바쁜 척했어요.

(= He/she kept calling me, so I just pretended I was busy.)

26. 아무리 추워 봤자 작년처럼 춥지는 않을 거예요.

(= No matter how cold it is, it will not be as cold as last year.)

Section V - Listening Comprehension

<Transcript>

여자: 우와! 현우 씨 그림 잘 그리시네요.

남자: 아니에요. 제가 아무리 잘 그려 봤자 경화 씨처럼은 못 그리죠.

여자: 네? 제 그림을 언제 보셨길래 제가 그림을 잘 그린다고 생각하세요?

남자: 이 그림 경화 씨가 그린 거 아니에요?

Woman: Wow! You are good at drawing!

Man: Not really. No matter how good I am at drawing, I can't draw as well as you.

Woman: Huh? When did you see my drawing that made you think I am good at drawing?

Man: Isn't this drawing drawn by you?

27. c

Section VI - Speaking Practice

여자: 우와! 현우 씨 그림 잘 그리시네요.

[우와! 혀누 씨 그림 잘 그리시네요.]

남자: 아니에요..

[아니에요.]

제가 아무리 잘 그려 봤자 경화 씨처럼은 못 그리죠.

[제가 아무리 잘 그려 봗짜 경화 씨처러믄 몯 끄리조.]

여자: 네? 제 그림을 언제 보셨길래 제가 그림을 잘 그린다

고 생각하세요?

[네? 제 그리믈 언제 보션낄래 제가 그리믈 잘 그린다

고 생가카세요?]

남자: 이 그림 경화 씨가 그린 거 아니에요?

[이 그림 경화 씨가 그린 거 아니에요?]

Lesson 11

Section I - Vocabulary

1. a   2. g   3. f   4. d

5. c   6. e   7. b

Section II - Comprehension

8. 아빠가 아기를 재우고 있어요.

(= A dad is putting his baby to sleep.)

9. 동생에게 티셔츠를 입혔어요.

(= I dressed my younger brother/sister in a t-

shirt.)

10. 선생님이 학생에게 책을 읽혔어요.

(= A teacher had his/her student read a book.)

11. 컵에 물을 좀 채워 주세요.

(= Please fill the cup with water.)

12. 동생이 신발을 잘 못 신어서 제가 신겨 줬어요.

(= My younger brother/sister was struggling with

putting on shoes, so I put them on for him/her.)

13. 의자가 너무 높은데, 낮춰 줄 수 있어요?

(= The chair is too high. Can you lower it?)

14. 책상이 너무 낮으니까 좀 높여 주세요.

(= The desk is too low, so please raise it.)

15. 친구에게 제 남편 사진을 보여 줬어요.

(= I showed my friend a picture of my husband.)

16. 아이들 울리지 마세요.

(= Don't make the kids cry.)

17. 음악 소리가 너무 작은데, 좀 키워 줄래요?

(= The music is too quiet. Can you turn it up?)

18. 음식을 남기지 마세요.

(= Don't leave food (on your plate).)

19. 엄마가 아기에게 밥을 먹여 줬어요.

(= A mom fed her baby.)

20. 눈이 많이 와서 선생님이 학생들을 집에 가게 했어요.

(= Since it snowed a lot, the teacher let the stu-

dents go home.)

21. 집이 너무 더러워서 친구를 못 오게 했어요.

(= Because my house was too dirty, I didn't let

my friend come over.)

22. 제가 좀 늦었죠? 오래 기다리게 해서 미안해요.

(= I'm a little late, aren't I? Sorry for making you

wait so long.)

23. 체육 선생님이 우리를 뛰게 했어요.

(= The P.E. teacher made us run.)

24. 선생님이 저를 TTMIK 책으로 공부시켰어요.

(= My teacher had me study with TTMIK books.)

25. 자, 공연이 곧 시작됩니다. 가수들을 준비시키세요.

(= The performance starts soon. Get the singers ready.)

Section III - Complete the Diary

<Translation>

My family consists of my mom, dad, me, and my

younger sister. We are also [26.] raising one cat. My

sister is only four years old, so I have to help out

my parents. This evening, because my mom and

dad were busy, only my sister and I were at home. I

[27.] put my sister in a chair, but the chair was too low,

so I [28.] raised it a bit. And I [29.] fed her bibimbap, but

she [30.] left all the vegetables because she doesn't

like vegetables. When it turned 9 p.m., she started

crying. I [31.] washed her and [32.] put her pajamas on.

Then I [33.] put her to sleep by reading a fairy tale

book to her.

26. 키우고 있다   27. 앉혔는데   28. 높였다

29. 먹여 줬다   30. 남겼다   31. 씻기고

32. 입혔다   33. 재웠다

34. <u>다른 것도 보여 주세요</u>

    (= Show me some other things too.)

35. <u>아이들 울리지 마세요</u>

    (= Don't make the kids cry.)

Section V - Listening Comprehension

\<Transcript\>

남자: 하은이는 진짜 순한 아이 같아요. 하은이처럼 순하면 열 명도 키우겠어요.

여자: 하은이요? 평소에는 순한데 재울 때 너무 힘들어요.

남자: 왜요?

여자: 침대에 눕히려고 하면 울어요. 그래서 매일 업고 재워서 허리가 너무 아파요.

Man: Ha-eun seems like such a mild-mannered kid. If my kids were mild-mannered like Ha-eun, I could even raise ten of them.

Woman: Ha-eun? She is usually mild-mannered, but when I put her to sleep, it is really difficult.

Man: Why?

Woman: If I am about to lay her on the bed, she cries. So my back hurts a lot because I put her to sleep by piggyback every day.

36. c   37. d

Section VI - Speaking Practice

남자: 하은이는 진짜 순한 아이 같아요.

    [하으니는 진짜 순한 아이 가타요.]

    하은이처럼 순하면 열 명도 키우겠어요.

    [하으니처럼 순하면 열 명도 키우게써요.]

여자: 하은이요?

    [하으니요?]

    평소에는 순한데 재울 때 너무 힘들어요.

    [평소에는 순한데 재울 때 너무 힘드러요.]

남자: 왜요?

    [왜요?]

여자: 침대에 눕히려고 하면 울어요.

    [침대에 누피려고 하면 우러요.]

    그래서 매일 업고 재워서 허리가 너무 아파요.

    [그래서 매일 업꼬 재워서 허리가 너무 아파요.]

Lesson 12

Section I - Vocabulary

1. to not know

2. to dye, to color

3. to ask

4. to be hot

5. to be busy

6. (police) detective, (police) investigator

7. to be pleased, to be glad

8. to grieve, to feel sad

9. concert

10. to press, to push

11. to be interesting/amazing

12. to get used to

Section II - Conjugation Practice

13. 아까 집에 <u>가더라고요</u>.

    (= I saw him leaving for home earlier.)

14. 당연하지. 진짜 <u>재미있더라고</u>.

    (= Of course. I found it really fun.)

15. 좋았어요. 특히 <u>바다가 정말 예쁘더라고요</u>.

    (= It was good. Especially, the beach was really pretty.)

16. 매울 줄 알았는데 <u>생각보다 안 맵더라고</u>.

    (= I thought it would be hot, but it was not as spicy as I thought.)

17. 그럴 줄 알았어. 석진이가 <u>공부를 열심히 하더라고</u>.

    (= I knew it. I saw him studying hard.)

18. 네, <u>빨간색이 잘 어울리더라고요</u>.

    (= Yes, she looked good with red hair.)

    [왜요?]

여자: 침대에 눕히려고 하면 울어요.

    [침대에 누피려고 하면 우러요.]

    그래서 매일 업고 재워서 허리가 너무 아파요.

    [그래서 매일 업꼬 재워서 허리가 너무 아파요.]

Section III - Reading Comprehension

<Translation>

When I first came to Korea, there were a lot of things that I found interesting. I went to a restaurant, and there was a button on the table, so I pressed it and a server ⑤ came over. It was very nice and convenient. Also, I knew that Koreans eat a lot of kimchi, but I didn't know the fact that they eat it every day. I came to learn that here. A friend of mine says that she even has a kimchi refrigerator. Also, ⑥ there were so many cafes on the street. At the time I thought, "Wow, Korean people really ⑥ love coffee!" However, I don't find such things interesting now. I've been living here for a long time, so I got used to it.

19. d   20. c

Section IV - Dictation

21. 싱가포르에 처음 가 봤는데, 정말 덥더라.

(= I went to Singapore for the first time, and it's really hot there.)

22. 아까 주연 씨 만났는데, 친구랑 있더라고.

(= I met Jooyeon earlier, and she was with her friend.)

23. 윤아 씨한테 물어봤는데, 모르더라고요.

(= I asked Yoona, and she did not know.)

Section V - Listening Comprehension

<Transcript>

여자: 오늘 오랜만에 홍대 갔는데, 그 카페 없어졌더라.

남자: 무슨 카페?

여자 : 네가 자주 가는 카페 있잖아.

남자: 어? 왜 갑자기 없어졌지?

여자: 글쎄. 오늘 보니까 없더라고.

Woman: I went to Hongdae today for the first time

in a long time, and the café was gone.

Man: Which café?

Woman: You know, the café where you often go.

Man: Huh? Why is it gone all of a sudden?

Woman: I don't know. I looked for it today, and it wasn't there.

24. d   25. a

Section VI - Speaking Practice

여자: 오늘 오랜만에 홍대 갔는데, 그 카페 없어졌더라.

[오늘 오랜마네 홍대 간는데, 그 까페* 업써젇떠라.]

남자: 무슨 카페?

[무슨 까페?]

여자: 네가 자주 가는 카페 있잖아.

[니가 자주 가는 까페 읻짜나.]

남자: 어? 왜 갑자기 없어졌지?

[어? 왜 갑짜기 업써젇찌?]

여자: 글쎄.

[글쎄.]

오늘 보니까 없더라고.

[오늘 보니까 업떠라고.]

* 카페 is technically pronounced [카페], but most people pronounce it [까페].

Lesson 13

Section I - Vocabulary

1. 제습기 dehumidifier

2. 건조기 dryer

3. 발전기 electric generator

4. 전화기 telephone

5. 계산기 calculator

6. 교육 기관 educational organization

7. 비행기 airplane

8. 자판기 vending machine

9. 복사기 copy machine, photocopier

10. 세탁기 washing machine

11. 선풍기 electric fan

12. 언론 기관 the media, the press

13. 청소기 vacuum cleaner

14. 정부 기관 government organization

Section II - Comprehension

15. d   16. b   17. c   18. d   19. a

Section III - Dictation

20. 세탁기 새로 샀어요? 좋은데요!

(= Did you buy a new washing machine? It looks nice!)

21. 저희 선풍기도 생겼어요.

(= We also have an electric fan now.)

Section IV - Listening Comprehension

<Transcript>

남자: 복사기 새로 샀어요? 좋은데요!

여자: 네. 저희 자판기도 생겼어요.

남자: 우와. 어디에 있어요?

여자: 지민 씨 뒤에 있어요.

Man: Did you buy a new copy machine? It looks nice!

Woman: Yes. We also have a vending machine now.

Man: Wow. Where is it?

Woman: It's behind you.

22. d   23. a

Section V - Speaking Practice

남자: 복사기 새로 샀어요?

[복싸기 새로 사써요?]

좋은데요!

[조은데요!]

여자: 네. 저희 자판기도 생겼어요.

[네. 저히 자판기도 생겨써요.]

남자: 우와. 어디에 있어요?

[우와. 어디에 이써요?]

여자: 지민 씨 뒤에 있어요.

[지민 씨 뒤에 이써요.]

Lesson 14

Section I - Vocabulary

1. No matter how difficult it is

2. No matter how expensive it is

3. No matter how delicious it is

4. No matter how busy you are

5. No matter how much you hate it

6. No matter how much I study

7. No matter how rich you are

8. No matter how kind the staff is

Section II - Complete the Sentence

9. 아무리 바빠도 부모님에게 자주 전화하려고 해요.

(= No matter how busy I am, I try to call my parents often.)

10. 제가 아무리 바보여도/바보라도 이 정도는 알죠.

(= No matter how big of a fool I am, I know this much, of course.)

11. 시험이 아무리 어려워도 포기하지 마세요.

(= No matter how difficult the exam is, don't give up.)

12. 아무리 비싸도 맛있으면 괜찮아.

(= No matter how expensive it is, if it's delicious, that's okay.)

13. 아무리 선생님이어도/선생님이라도 실수할 때가 있어요.

(= Even if you are a teacher, you sometimes make mistakes.)

14. 아무리 추워도 눈이 오면 기분이 좋아요.

(= No matter how cold it is, I feel good if it snows.)

15. 돈이 아무리 많아도 친구가 없으면 행복하지 않을 거야.

(= No matter how much money you have, you will

not feel happy if you don't have friends.)

16. 이 노래는 아무리 들어도 좋아요.

(= No matter how many times I listen to this

song, it sounds good.)

17. 아무리 먹어도 배가 안 부르네요.

(= No matter how much I eat, I don't feel full.)

18. 이 영화는 아무리 봐도 지겹지 않아. 너무 재미있어.

(= No matter how many times I watch this movie,

I don't find it boring. It's so fun.)

Section III - Reading Comprehension

<Translation>

Jina: I'm learning to code these days.

Sohee: Really? Why?

Jina: Because I'm staying home all the time, I'm so

bored.

Sohee: ___①___ Why coding?

Jina: I guess you don't know. There are so many peo-

ple who are learning to code these days. Even

elementary school students learn. However, to

me, ___①___ I guess I'm a fool.

19. d   20. a

Section IV - Dictation

21. 아무리 늦어도 두 시까지는 오세요.

(= Come by two o'clock at the latest.)

22. 아무리 학생이라도 공부만 하는 건 아니에요.

(= Even students do not always study.)

Section V - Listening Comprehension

<Transcript>

여자: 이 식당은 너무 불친절한 것 같아요.

남자: 맞아요. 너무 심하네요.

여자: 저는 음식이 아무리 맛있어도 불친절한 식당은

다시 오고 싶지 않아요.

남자: 그래요? 저는 아무리 친절해도 음식이 맛없으면

다시 안 가요.

Woman: I think the people in this restaurant are

very rude.

Man: That's right. They are very rude.

Woman: I don't want to go to rude restaurants again

no matter how good the food is.

Man: Is that so? I don't go to restaurants again if the

food is not good no matter how kind they are.

23. a   24. d

Section VI - Speaking Practice

여자: 이 식당은 너무 불친절한 것 같아요.

[이 식땅은 너무 불친절한 건 가타요.]

남자: 맞아요.

[마자요.]

너무 심하네요.

[너무 심하네요.]

여자: 저는 음식이 아무리 맛있어도 불친절한 식당은 다시

오고 싶지 않아요.

[저는 음시기 아무리 마시써도 불친절한 식땅은 다시

오고 십찌 아나요.]

남자: 그래요?

[그래요?]

저는 아무리 친절해도 음식이 맛없으면 다시 안 가요.

[저는 아무리 친절해도 음시기 마덥쓰면 다시 안 가요.]

Lesson 15

Section I - Vocabulary

1. 싫어하다   2. 모든   3. 이름

4. 끝내다   5. 생일   6. 출발하다

7. 어떤   8. 약속하다   9. 돌아가다

Section II - Comprehension

10. 우리 약속한 날이 언제였죠?

11. 이게 한국말로 뭐였죠?

12. 경화 생일이 몇 월이더라? or 경화 생일이 몇 월이었지?

13. 캐시가 어느 나라 사람이라고 했죠?

14. 현우 씨가 언제 한국에 돌아간다고 했죠?

15. 경복궁에 어떻게 간다고 하더라? or 경복궁에 어떻게 간다고 했지? (경복궁에 어떻게 간다고 했더라? is also possible.)

Section III - Complete the Dialogue

16. b

Hyunwoo: Kyeong-eun, what was your friend's name again who we met last week?

Kyeong-eun: Oh, you mean Seokjin?

17. a

Hyunwoo: When are we supposed to leave? (I forgot⋯)

Kyeong-eun: Let's leave at five o'clock.

18. b

Jooyeon: Where should we meet?

Kyeong-eun: Let's meet in front of the office.

19. a

Hyunwoo: Where is the cafe? (I forgot⋯)

Kyeong-eun: Come on, it's next to the park.

20. c

Dahye: Manager, when do I have to do this by?

Manager: You can finish it by next week.

Section IV - Dictation

21. 언제 온다고 했죠?

(= When did they say they were going to come?)

22. 이거 누구 거라고 했더라?

(= Whose did you say this was?)

Section V - Listening Comprehension

<Transcript>

남자: 경화 씨가 싫어하는 아이스크림이 뭐였죠?

여자: 경화 씨는 아이스크림 다 좋아해요.

남자: 아니에요. 어떤 아이스크림 안 좋아한다고 했는데... 뭐더라?

여자: 아! 기억났어요. 바닐라 아이스크림 안 좋아한다고 했어요.

Man: What was the ice cream that Kyung-hwa dislikes?

Woman: Kyung-hwa likes all kinds of ice cream.

Man: No. She said she doesn't like some kind of ice cream. What was it?

Woman: Oh! I remember! She said she doesn't like vanilla ice cream.

23. d   24. c

Section VI - Speaking Practice

남자: 경화 씨가 싫어하는 아이스크림이 뭐였죠?

[경화 씨가 시러하는 아이스크리미 뭐엳쪼?]

여자: 경화 씨는 아이스크림 다 좋아해요.

[경화 씨는 아이스크림 다 조아해요.]

남자: 아니에요.

[아니에요.]

어떤 아이스크림 안 좋아한다고 했는데...

[어떤 아이스크림 안 조아한다고 핸는데⋯]

뭐더라?

[뭐더라?]

여자: 아! 기억났어요.

[아! 기엉나써요.]

바닐라 아이스크림 안 좋아한다고 했어요.

[바닐라 아이스크림 안 조아한다고 해써요.]

Lesson 16

Section I - Vocabulary

1. f   2. c   3. g   4. d

5. b   6. a   7. h   8. e

Section II - Translation Practice

9. 매일 운동한다니까요.

10. 공부 좀 하라니까요!

11. 다음 주부터 열심히 공부할 거라니까요! or 다음 주부터 열심히 공부한다니까요!

12. (저는) 정말/진짜 몰랐다니까요.

13. 빨리 오라니까요.

14. 알았다니까요! or 알겠다니까요!

15. 이거 안 하고 싶다니까요.

16. 혼자 갈 거라니까요! or 혼자 간다니까요!

Section III - Reading Comprehension

<Translation>

To Mark

Hi, thanks for the letter.

I see you have learned -다니까(요). It's a good expression!

However, you have to be a little careful when using this expression.

If you use this expression too often, you sound like a person who doesn't like saying the same thing several times.

So the listener might be offended.

When you talk to someone who you have met for the first time, who is older than you, or who you are not close to, be careful.

If you have something else you don't know, ask me anytime! :)

Okay, bye!

Hyunwoo

17. c   18. d

Section IV - Dictation

19. 일 있어서 못 내려간다니까.

(= I said I can't go down because I've got something to do.)

20. 그럴 수도 있다니까요.

(= I said it is also possible.)

Section V - Listening Comprehension

<Transcript>

여자: 추석 기차표 예매했어?

남자: 이번 추석에 일 있어서 못 내려간다니까.

여자: 나 혼자 갈 거라니까.

남자: 그럼 네가 예매해.

Woman: Have you booked the train tickets for Chuseok?

Man: I said I can't go this Chuseok because I've got something to do.

Woman: I told you I would go by myself.

Man: Then you book your ticket.

21. c   22. b

Section VI - Speaking Practice

여자: 추석 기차표 예매했어?

[추석 기차표 예매해써?]

남자: 이번 추석에 일 있어서 못 내려간다니까.

[이번 추서게 이리써서 몬내려간다니까.]

여자: 나 혼자 갈 거라니까.

[나 혼자 갈 꺼라니까.]

남자: 그럼 네가 예매해.

[그럼 니가 예매해.]

Lesson 17

Section I - Vocabulary

1. g   2. d   3. f   4. e   5. i

6. c   7. b   8. h   9. a   10. j

11. 팔았대요 - 판대요 - 팔 거래요

12. 아팠대요 - 아프대요 - 아플 거래요

13. 바빴대요 - 바쁘대요 - 바쁠 거래요

14. 추웠대요 - 춥대요 - 추울 거래요

15. 유명했대요 - 유명하대요 - 유명할 거래요

16. 끝났대요 - 끝난대요 - 끝날 거래요

17. 이사 갔대요 - 이사 간대요 - 이사 갈 거래요

18. 없었대요 - 없대요 - 없을 거래요

19. 친구였대요 - 친구래요 - 친구일 거래요

20. 마지막이었대요 - 마지막이래요 - 마지막일 거래요

Section III - Reading Comprehension

<Translation>

Today, it snowed a lot in Seoul. Buses were also late because of the bad road conditions. Some people couldn't go home because they got stuck in traffic. However, there were people who liked the sudden snow. They were children. Children made snowmen and took pictures. Adults suffered, but children were happy.

21. d   22. b

Section IV - Dictation

23. 주연 씨가 말한 <u>연고 안 판대요</u>.

(= They said that they don't sell the ointment Jooyeon talked about.)

24. 거기는 <u>그 연고 없대요</u>.

(= They said that they don't have the ointment.)

Section V - Listening Comprehension

<Transcript>

남자: 약국에서 주연 씨가 말한 연고 안 판대요.

여자: 저쪽 코너에 있는 약국 갔어요?

남자: 네. 거기는 그 연고 없대요.

여자: 거기 말고 병원 바로 옆에 있는 약국으로 가 보세요. 거기는 팔 거예요.

Man: At the pharmacy, they said that they don't sell the ointment you talked about.

Woman: Did you go to the pharmacy on the corner over there?

Man. Yes. They said that they don't have the ointment.

Woman: Then go to the pharmacy right next to the hospital, not that one. They should sell it.

25. b   26. c

Section VI - Speaking Practice

남자: 약국에서 주연 씨가 말한 연고 안 판대요.

[약꾸게서 주연 씨가 말한 연고 안 판대요.]

여자: 저쪽 코너에 있는 약국 갔어요?

[저쪽 코너에 인는 약꾹 가써요?]

남자: 네. 거기는 그 연고 없대요.

[네. 거기는 그 연고 업때요.]

여자: 거기 말고 병원 바로 옆에 있는 약국으로 가 보세요.

[거기 말고 병원 바로 여페 인는 약꾸그로 가 보세요.]

거기는 팔 거예요.

[거기는 팔 꺼예요.]

Lesson 18

Section I - Vocabulary

1. to arrive   2. later   3. by oneself

4. last week   5. next year   6. new

7. laptop   8. to cut   9. to be dangerous

10. not (so) much

Section II - Contraction Practice

11. 눈이 왔다던데요

12. 머리를 자른다던데요

13. 학교에 안 갈 거라던데요

14. 대학생이라던데요

15. 여행 갔다던데요

16. 거기 위험하다던데요

Section III - Comprehension

17. 경화가 새 노트북 샀다던데, 물어봐.

    (= Kyung-hwa said that she bought a new laptop.
    Ask her.)

18. 지나는 이따가 드라마 봐야 된다던데.

    (= Jina said that she has to watch a drama later
    today.)

19. 희주도 내년부터 (진짜) 운동할 거라던데, 같이 하면
    되겠네.

    (= Heeju said that she would work out starting
    next year. I think you can do it with her.)

20. 아니. 윤아가 그 영화 (봤는데,) 별로 재미없었다던데.

    (재미없다던데 is also possible.)

    (= No. Yoona said that she watched it, but it was
    not really enjoyable.)

21. 석진이는 좀 늦을 것 같다던데.

    (= Seokjin said that he might be a little late.)

22. 승완이 핸드폰이라던데.

    (= I heard that it is Seung-wan's mobile phone.)

Section IV - Dictation

23. 이번 학교 축제 때 유명한 가수 온다던데?

    (= I heard that a famous singer is coming to our
    upcoming school festival.)

24. 가수는 아무도 안 올 거라던데?

    (= I heard that no singers would come.)

Section V - Listening Comprehension

<Transcript>

남자: 이번 학교 축제 때 유명한 가수 온다던데?

여자: 아니야. 가수는 아무도 안 올 거라던데?

남자: 아무도 안 온다고? 설마.

여자: 진짜야.

Man: I heard that a famous singer is coming to our
     upcoming school festival.

Woman: No. I heard that no singers will come.

Man: You're saying no singers will come? No way.

Woman: I'm serious.

25. d   26. a

Section VI - Speaking Practice

남자: 이번 학교 축제 때 유명한 가수 온다던데?

    [이번 학꾜 축쩨 때 유명한 가수 온다던데?]

여자: 아니야. 가수는 아무도 안 올 거라던데?

    [아니야. 가수는 아무도 아놀꺼라던데?]

남자: 아무도 안 온다고? 설마.

    [아무도 아논다고? 설마.]

여자: 진짜야.

    [진짜야.]

Lesson 19

Section I - Vocabulary

1. e	2. i	3. f	4. j	5. h
6. c	7. a	8. b	9. g	10. d

Section II - Translation Practice

11. 몇 시에 올 거냐고 물어보세요

12. 왜 안 왔냐고 물어봤어요

13. 저한테 어디 가냐고 물어봤어요

14. 누가 그렇게 말했냐고 물어봤어요

15. 저한테 몇 살이냐고 물어봤어요

16. 저한테 결혼했냐고 물어보지 마세요

17. 선생님한테 이번 시험이 얼마나 어렵냐고 물어봤어요

18. 어린 것 같아서 학생이냐고 물어봤어요. or 어리다고
    생각해서 학생이냐고 물어봤어요

19. 친구한테 어디에서 옷을 샀냐고 물어봤어요 (어디서
    is also possible.)

20. 친구가 저한테 이번 주말에 뭐 할 거냐고 물어봤어요

    * All 물어보다 above can be replaced with 묻다 or
    질문하다, but 물어보다 is the most commonly
    used expression with the meaning of "to ask".

Section III - Reading Comprehension

<Translation>

Hi, guys. I came to Korea last week.

By the way, why do Koreans always ask me how old I am?

∟ It's because age matters in Korea because of the casual and polite speaking styles.

∟ True. And Koreans also ask if you are married a lot.

∟ Lol I've been asked too. Or a lot of people ask when you will get married too.

∟ Right. And there are also a lot of people who ask what your blood type is.

∟ It's interesting that Koreans know their blood type.

∟ Agreed. But it seems that people talk about MBTI more often than blood types these days.

21. a   22. b

Section IV - Dictation

23. 몇 살이냐고 물어봤어요.

(= They asked me how old I was.)

24. 저한테 언제 가냐고 물었어요.

(= They asked me when I was going.)

Section V - Listening Comprehension

<Transcript>

남자: 한국 사람들은 왜 항상 밥 먹었냐고 물어봐요?

여자: 한국 사람들한테는 그게 인사예요.

남자: 밥 말고 다른 거 먹었으면 뭐라고 말해요?

여자: 그냥 먹었다고 하면 돼요. 뭐 먹었냐고 물어보는 거 아니에요.

Man: Why do Korean people always ask if you have eaten rice?

Woman: To Korean people, that is a greeting.

Man: If I had something else rather than rice, what should I say?

Woman: You can just say you have eaten. It's not that they're asking what you ate.

25. d   26. d

Section VI - Speaking Practice

남자: 한국 사람들은 왜 항상 밥 먹었냐고 물어봐요?

[한국 사람드른 왜 항상 밤머건냐고 무러봐요?]

여자: 한국 사람들한테는 그게 인사예요.

[한국 사람들한테는 그게 인사예요.]

남자: 밥 말고 다른 거 먹었으면 뭐라고 말해요?

[밤말고 다른 거 머거쓰면 뭐라고 말해요?]

여자: 그냥 먹었다고 하면 돼요.

[그냥 머걷따고 하면 돼요.]

뭐 먹었냐고 물어보는 거 아니에요.

[뭐 머건냐고 무러보는 거 아니에요.]

Lesson 20

Section I - Vocabulary

| 1. b | 2. g | 3. d | 4. j | 5. c |
| 6. h | 7. f | 8. a | 9. e | 10. i |

Section II - Conjugation Practice

11. 어제 친구랑 영화를 봤는데, 사람이 정말 많더라고요.

= I saw a movie with my friend yesterday, and there were so many people there.

12. 그 책 읽었는데, 정말 재미있더라고요.

= I read that book, and I found it really enjoyable.

13. 석진 씨한테 물어봤는데, 잘 모르더라고요.

= I asked Seokjin, but he didn't really know about it.

14. 냉장고 문을 열었는데, 우유가 없더라고요.

= I opened the refrigerator door, and (I saw that) there was no milk.

15. 이메일 답장한 다음에 친구 만난대요.

= He/she says he/she is going to meet his/her friends after he/she replies to the email.

16. 집에 간 다음에 전화한대요.

= He/she says he/she is going to make a phone call after he/she gets home.

17. 일 끝난 다음에 영화 본대요.

= He/she says he/she is going to watch a movie after he/she finishes work.

18. 아무리 피곤해도 커피를 그렇게 많이 마시면 안 돼요.

= No matter how tired you are, you should not drink that much coffee.

19. 아무리 날씨가 추워도 늦으면 안 돼요.

= No matter how cold the weather is, you should not be late.

20. 아무리 바빠도 그거 잊어버리면 안 돼요.

= No matter how busy you are, you should not forget that.

Section III - Reading Comprehension

<Translation>

Kyeong-eun: Hello, nice to meet you. Your Korean is amazing, how did you study?

Cassie: Of course with "Talk To Me In Korean". My friend bought the Talk To Me In Korean book first, and he said he found it 21. good. So, I bought it too.

Kyeong-eun: I see. Wasn't Korean difficult?

Cassie: Well, it was a bit difficult, but I found it fun because it's different from English. That's why, 22. no matter how busy I was, I studied for at least 30 minutes every day.

Kyeong-eun: Awesome. Did you happen to have something especially memorable happen when in Korea?

Cassie: A lot. Something funny happened because of age. When I first came to Korea, Koreans often asked me 23. how old I was. But you know, in Korea, people calculate their age differently than other countries. At first, I didn't know, so... 24. what was it? (I forgot.) What was "international age'" in Korean

again?

Kyeong-eun: You mean 만 나이?

Cassie: Oh, yes! 만 나이. So I said I was 26, which was my international age. And then, my friend, who was 28 years old, 25. told me to call him 오빠. So I kept calling him 오빠. However, about a year later, we had a chance to ask each other when we were born, and we found out that we were born in the same year. I had called him 오빠 for a year until then! It was hilarious.

Kyeong-eun: It really is. That's why it's a bit complicated when Koreans talk about their age with people from other countries.

Cassie: Right. It's really 26. complicated, as I said.

21. 좋았대요   22. 아무리 바빠도

23. 몇 살이냐고   24. 뭐더라

25. 하더라고요   26. 복잡하다니까요

Section IV - Dictation

27. 어제 주연 씨를 만났는데, 머리를 빨간색으로 염색했더라고요.

(= I met Jooyeon yesterday, and you know what, I saw that she had dyed her hair red.)

28. 아무리 화가 나도 혼자 가면 안 돼요.

(= No matter how upset you are, you should not go there alone.)

Section V - Listening Comprehension

<Transcript>

남자: 경화 씨, 주연 씨한테 전화해 보세요.

여자: 아까 전화했는데 안 받더라고요.

남자: 그래요? 다시 한 번 해 보세요.

여자: 네. (잠시 후) 아무리 해도 안 받아요.

Man: Kyung-hwa, try calling Jooyeon.

Woman: I called her earlier, but she didn't answer.

Man: She didn't? Please try calling her again.

Woman: Okay. (A little later) No matter how many times I do, she doesn't answer.

29. d   30. a

Section VI - Speaking Practice

남자: 경화 씨, 주연 씨한테 전화해 보세요.

    [경화 씨, 주연 씨한테 전화해 보세요.]

여자: 아까 전화했는데 안 받더라고요.

    [아까 전화핸는데 안 받떠라고요.]

남자: 그래요? 다시 한 번 해 보세요.

    [그래요? 다시 한 번 해 보세요.]

여자: 네. (잠시 후)

    [네.]

아무리 해도 안 받아요.

    [아무리 해도 안 바다요.]

Lesson 21

Section I - Vocabulary

1. g   2. h   3. f   4. j   5. a

6. c   7. b   8. i   9. e   10. d

Section II - Conjugation Practice

11. 다혜 씨가 서점에 가잖아요

12. 다혜 씨가 서점에 간다잖아요

13. 밖에 비가 오고 있었잖아요

14. 밖에 비가 오고 있었다잖아요

15. 이거 석준 씨 옷이잖아요

16. 이거 석준 씨 옷이라잖아요

17. 소희 씨 생일이 이번 주 토요일이잖아요

18. 소희 씨 생일이 이번 주 토요일이라잖아요

19. 그건 10년 전이었잖아요

20. 그건 10년 전이었다잖아요

Section III - Reading Comprehension

21. 실패는 성공의 어머니라잖아요

22. 급할수록 천천히 가라잖아요

23. 노력하면 못 할 것이 없다잖아요

<Translation>

TTMIK Counseling center

21. Hello! I'm a student who is studying the Korean language.

I studied Korean for two years, but I still make a lot of mistakes when speaking in Korean. ㅠ_ㅠ

How do you think I can not make mistakes?

I really want to be good at Korean!!!!

comments ㄴ daniel.0610: Wow, you are good at Korean!!! ^0^

    ㄴ thisisyou: It's okay to make mistakes! You know, people say failure is the mother of success. The more mistakes you make, the more you will learn.

22. I'm a 28 year old woman. Recently, I got a job in a new company.

Therefore, I'm looking for (housing) in order to move close to the company.

But the landlord of one place is pushing me to sign the contract as soon as possible, so I feel rushed. Do you think I should sign the contract quickly?

comments ㄴ thisisyou: I think you should take your time! You know, people say more haste, less speed.

    ㄴ nicerrrr: If the room is good, go sign the contract quickly. Someone might sign the contract first.

    ㄴ coco_5: Take your time thinking and decide.

23. I'm a high school boy.

I'd like to learn a lot of languages, but I find it too difficult even though I'm only learning English now.

Nevertheless, I'd like to learn about five languages. Do you think I can?

comments └, nerdynerd._.: I studied three languages, but it was so difficult! ㅠ_ㅠ
Cheer up!

└, thisisyou: Yes, of course you can! You
know, people say if you make the
effort, there is nothing you can't do.

└, love.237: Which language are you
going to study?

Section IV - Dictation

24. 커피보다 차가 건강에 더 좋다잖아요.

(= Come on, people say tea is better for your
health than coffee.)

25. 그 책을 쓴 사람이 현우 씨라잖아요.

(= Didn't you hear that the person who wrote the
book is Hyunwoo?)

Section V - Listening Comprehension

\<Transcript>

남자: 캐시 씨, 점심 같이 먹을래요?

여자1: 아니요. 저는 혼자 먹을게요.

남자: 같이 먹어요.

여자2: 캐시 씨가 혼자 먹겠다잖아요. 현우 씨랑 같이
먹기 싫다잖아요.

Man: Cassie, do you want to have lunch with us?

Woman1: No. I will eat on my own.

Man: Let's have lunch together.

Woman2: Didn't you hear Cassie say she would eat
by herself? Come on, she said that she
doesn't want to eat with you!

26. c

Section VI - Speaking Practice

남자: 캐시 씨, 점심 같이 먹을래요?

[캐씨 씨, 점심 가치 머글래요?]

여자1: 아니요. 저는 혼자 먹을게요.

[아니요. 저는 혼자 머글께요.]

남자: 같이 먹어요.

[가치 머거요.]

여자2: 캐시 씨가 혼자 먹겠다잖아요.

[캐씨 씨가 혼자 먹껜따자나요.]

현우 씨랑 같이 먹기 싫다잖아요.

[혀누 씨랑 가치 먹끼 실타자나요.]

Lesson 22

Section I - Vocabulary

1. f	2. k	3. g	4. o	5. n
6. a	7. l	8. b	9. i	10. d
11. j	12. e	13. c	14. m	15. h

Section II - Comprehension

16. b

What do you want to eat? You decide.

17. a

This flight will soon be arriving at Incheon International Airport.

18. b

You were very surprised, right? Get some rest.

19. c

I get up at a set time every day.

20. a

It's my fault. I'll admit it. I'm sorry.

Section III - Fill in the Blank

<Translation>

Yo, What's up?

Let me ^{21.} officially introduce myself. Everyone, stay tuned.

Rapping in Korean from now on is my ^{22.} plan.

Which word should I use? That's a very difficult ^{23.} decision.

I think and confirm (what to use) out of many words.

As soon as you listen to my rap, you feel ^{24.} calm.

And then (you'll) ^{25.} admit that I am the best, yeah.

No matter how hard you try, I win ^{26.} by point count~

21. 정식   22. 예정   23. 결정
24. 안정   25. 인정   26. 판정

Section IV - Dictation

27. 이 식당은 10년 동안 가격이 일정해요.

    (= The price has been constant for ten years in this restaurant.)

28. 이 옷은 정가가 십만 원인데 세일하고 있어요.

    (= The official price of this clothing item is 100,000 won, but it is on sale.)

Section V - Listening Comprehension

<Transcript>

여자: 어떤 옷 살 거예요?

남자: 아직 결정 못 했어요.

여자: 이 옷은 정가가 십만 원인데 팔십 프로 세일해서 이만 원이래요.

남자: 우와! 저 그 옷 살래요.

Woman: Which clothes are you going to buy?

Man: I haven't decided yet.

Woman: It says that the official price of this cloth-ing item is 100,000 won, but it is 80% off,

so it is 20,000 won.

Man: Wow! I will buy that clothing item.

29. F   30. T

Section VI - Speaking Practice

여자: 어떤 옷 살 거예요?

   [어떠놋 살 꺼예요?]

남자: 아직 결정 못 했어요.

   [아직 결쩡 모태써요.]

여자: 이 옷은 정가가 십만 원인데 팔십프로 세일해서 이만 원이래요.

   [이 오슨 정까가 심마눤인데 팔씹프로 쎄일해서 이마눠니래요.]

남자: 우와! 저 그 옷 살래요.

   [우와! 저 그옫 살래요.]

Lesson 23

Section I - Vocabulary

1. i   2. j   3. a   4. b   5. c
6. d   7. g   8. e   9. f   10. h

Section II - Comprehension

11. 물어보나 마나 늦는다고 할 거예요.

12. 이야기를 하나 마나 똑같을 거예요. (이야기하나 마나 is also possible.)

13. 그 영화 보나 마나예요. 내용이 뻔해요.

14. 보나 마나 경화 씨가 이길 거예요.

15. 제가 열심히 하나 마나 똑같을 거예요.

Section III - Complete the Dialogue

16. 들어 보나 마나

A: Have you listened to what Hyunwoo says?

B: No. Whether I listen to him or not, I think he will just make excuses.

17. 청소하나 마나

A: I'll clean this room.

B: Don't do it. Whether you clean it or not, it will be dirty.

18. 입으나 마나일

A: Wear these clothes if you feel cold.

B: These clothes? They are too thin, so I think they are worthless to wear.

19. 입이 보나 마나

A: Do you want to try on these clothes?

B: No. Whether I try them on or not, I think it will fit me perfectly.

20. 전화해 보나 마나예요

A: Do you think that restaurant is closed by now? Shall I call them?

B: It's worthless to call. It's 10 o'clock, so they are obviously closed.

Section IV - Dictation

21. 콜라를 그렇게 많이 마시면 <u>운동하나 마나예요</u>.

(= If you drink cola that much, your exercise becomes worthless.)

22. 저는 화장을 <u>하나 마나 똑같아요</u>.

(= Whether I wear makeup or not, I look the same.)

Section V - Listening Comprehension

<Transcript>

남자: 우리 볼링 시합할까요?

여자: 보나 마나 주연 씨가 일 등 하겠죠.

남자: 안 그럴 수도 있죠. 내기해요.

여자: 보나 마나예요.

Man: Shall we have a bowling match?

Woman: We don't have to. Jooyeon will be the winner.

Man: She might not be, right? Let's make a bet.

Woman: No need to.

23. a   24. c

Section VI - Speaking Practice

남자: 우리 볼링 시합할까요?

[우리 볼링 시하팔까요?]

여자: 보나 마나 주연 씨가 일 등 하겠죠.

[보나 마나 주연 씨가 일 뜽 하겓쪼.]

남자: 안 그럴 수도 있죠.

[안 그럴 쑤도 읻쪼.]

내기해요.

[내기해요.]

여자: 보나 마나예요.

[보나 마나예요.]

Lesson 24

Section I - Vocabulary

1. c	2. f	3. h	4. d	5. i
6. j	7. a	8. g	9. e	10. b

Section II - Comprehension

11. 책 두 권이 책상 위에 <u>놓여 있어요</u>.

(= Two books are put down on the desk.)

12. 창문이 <u>열려 있어요</u>.

(= The window is open.)

13. 옷이 의자 위에 <u>쌓여 있어요</u>.

(= The clothes are piled up on the chair.)

14. 컵이 바닥에 <u>깨져 있어요</u>.

(= The cup is broken on the floor.)

15. 에어컨이 <u>켜져 있어요</u>.

(= The air conditioner is turned on.)

Section III - Translation Practice

16. 창문이 깨져 있었어요

17. 불이 켜져 있어서 길이 or 불이 켜져 있어서 거리가

18. 잡혀 있어요

19. 산으로 둘러싸여 있어요

20. 담겨 있어요

Section IV - Dictation

21. 파란색으로 칠해져 있는 간판 <u>보여요</u>?

    (= Do you see the sign there that is painted in blue?)

22. 아침에 일어나니까 <u>눈이 쌓여 있었어요</u>.

    (= When I woke up this morning, I saw that the snow had piled up.)

Section V - Listening Comprehension

<Transcript>

여자: 오늘 점심 어디서 먹을까요?

남자: 라면집 옆에 있는 파스타집 갈까요?

여자: 거기는 점심때 문을 안 여나 봐요. 항상 닫혀 있 더라고요.

남자: 그래요? 어제 점심 시간에는 열려 있었어요. 한 번 가 봐요.

Woman: Where shall we have lunch today?

Man: Shall we go to the pasta place next to the ramyeon place?

Woman: I guess that place is not open for lunch. From what I've seen, it's always closed.

Man: Is that so? It was open at lunchtime yester-day. Let's check it out.

23. b   24. b

Section VI - Speaking Practice

여자: 오늘 점심 어디서 먹을까요?

    [오늘 점심 어디서 머글까요?]

남자: 라면집 옆에 있는 파스타집 갈까요?

    [라면찝 여페 인는 파스타찝 갈까요?]

여자: 거기는 점심때 문을 안 여나 봐요.

    [거기는 점심때 무늘 안 녀나 봐요.]

항상 닫혀 있더라고요.

[항상 다처 읻떠라고요.]

남자: 그래요?

[그래요?]

어제 점심 시간에는 열려 있었어요.

[어제 점심 시가네는 열려 이써써요.]

한번 가 봐요.

[한번 가 봐요.]

Lesson 25

Section I - Vocabulary

1. j   2. b   3. i   4. f   5. a

6. h   7. d   8. g   9. e   10. c

Section II - Complete the Dialogue, Part 1

11. 많이 먹으면 살이 찌게 되어 있어요

A: Why do I keep gaining weight?

B: If you eat a lot, you are bound to gain weight.

12. 몸을 많이 쓰면 잠이 잘 오게 되어 있어요

A: I can't sleep well these days.

B: You didn't move a lot during the day, right? If you use your body a lot, you are bound to fall asleep easily.

13. 운동을 하면 건강해지게 되어 있어요

A: I want to become healthy.

B: Exercise. If you exercise, you are bound to become healthy.

14. 봄이 오면 꽃이 피게 되어 있어요

A: When do you think flowers bloom?

B: I'm sure they will bloom soon. Spring is around

the corner. If spring comes, the flowers are bound to bloom.

15. 열심히 하면 언젠가 성공하게 되어 있어요

A: Do you think I can succeed?

B: Sure. If someone works hard like you, Hyunwoo, they are bound to succeed some day.

Section III - Complete the Dialogue, Part 2

16. 몸에서 멀어지면 마음에서도 멀어지게 되어 있더라고요

A: After my friend moved, I gradually didn't contact him/her often.

B: You know it's out of sight, out of mind.

17. 공짜라고 하면 다 좋아하게 되어 있더라고요

A: People really liked this.

B: Sure. It's free. If something is said to be free, everyone is bound to like it in my experience.

18. 매일 연습하면 잘 치게 되어 있더라고요

A: I also want to be good at playing the piano.

B: Try practicing every day. No matter how bad someone is at playing, if they practice every day, they are bound to be good at it in my experience.

19. 일찍 자면 일찍 일어나게 되어 있더라고요

A: How do you get up that much early, Joonbae?

B: I go to bed early. If you go to bed early, you are bound to get up early in my experience.

20. 서두르면 꼭 실수를 하게 되어 있더라고요

A: What time is it now? I should finish it quickly, right?

B: It's okay. Take your time. If you hurry, you are always bound to make mistakes in my experience.

Section IV - Dictation

21. 그건 어른이 되면 알게 되어 있어.

(= You will find out what it is when you become an adult.)

22. 만나야 할 사람들은 결국 만나게 되어 있어.

(= People who have to meet are bound to meet eventually.)

Section V - Listening Comprehension

<Transcript>

여자: 저는 글은 잘 쓰는데, 말은 잘 못하는 것 같아요.

남자: 아니에요. 글을 잘 쓰면 말도 잘하게 되어 있어요.

여자: 그냥 많이 하면 잘하게 될까요?

남자: 네. 연습을 많이 하면 늘게 되어 있어요.

Woman: I am good at writing, but I don't think I am good at speaking.

Man: That's not true. If you are good at writing, you are bound to be good at speaking as well.

Woman: Am I bound to get better at it if I do it a lot?

Man: I think so. You are bound to get better if you practice a lot.

23. b

Section VI - Speaking Practice

여자: 저는 글은 잘 쓰는데, 말은 잘 못하는 것 같아요.

[저는 그른 잘 쓰는데, 마른 잘 모타는 건 가타요.]

남자: 아니에요.

[아니에요.]

글을 잘 쓰면 말도 잘하게 되어 있어요.

[그를 잘 쓰면 말도 잘하게 되어 이써요.]

여자: 그냥 많이 하면 잘하게 될까요?

[그냥 마니 하면 잘하게 될까요?]

남자: 네. 연습을 많이 하면 늘게 되어 있어요.

　　[네. 연스블 마니 하면 늘게 되어 이써요.]

Lesson 26

Section I - Vocabulary

1. b　　2. e　　3. h　　4. a

5. d　　6. c　　7. g　　8. f

Section II - Comprehension

9. a

In addition to being big, that house is clean.

10. b

In addition to being pretty, that cake also tastes good.

11. c

In addition to being dirty, that room is small.

12. b

In addition to being tasty, this food is good for your health.

13. a

In addition to singing well, that singer also dances well.

Section III - Reading Comprehension

<Translation>

Hi!

I feel like I came back to Korea just a short time ago, but it's already been a year.

How are you doing? How's your college life?

In addition to having a nice personality, you are good at studying, so you're probably doing great, right?

Two years ago, you said you wanted to study Korean with Korean news, right?

That is why I'm sending you this book, News in Korean. I've found this book really good.

In addition to being fun and informative, it is also good when you prepare for the Korean exam. Try studying with this book thoroughly! :)

Okay, I will contact you again. Bye!

　　　　　　　　　　　　　　　　From Sohee

14. b　　15. c

Section IV - Dictation

16. 이 식당은 <u>시끄러운 데다가</u> 맛도 없어요.

　　(= In addition to being noisy, this restaurant's food is also not good.)

17. 다혜 씨는 <u>바쁜 데다가 하는 일도 많아서</u> 만나기 어려워요.

　　(= In addition to being busy, Dahye also does a lot of things, so it's difficult to meet her.)

Section V - Listening Comprehension

<Transcript>

남자: 어서 오세요.

여자: 안녕하세요.

남자: 여기가 좁은 골목에 있는 데다가 간판도 없어서 찾아오기 힘드셨죠?

여자: 네. 제가 길치인 데다가 홍대를 처음 와서 찾기 어렵더라고요.

Man: Welcome.

Woman: Hello.

Man: On top of being in a narrow alleyway, we also
     don't have a sign, so you must have had a
     hard time finding us, right?

Woman: Yes. On top of not being good with roads,
       this is my first time coming to Hongdae, so
       it was hard to find.

18. d

Section VI - Speaking Practice

남자: 어서 오세요.

   [어서 오세요.]

여자: 안녕하세요.

   [안녕하세요.]

남자: 여기가 좁은 골목에 있는 데다가 간판도 없어서 찾
   아오기 힘드셨죠?

   [여기가 조븐 골모게 인는 데다가 간판도 업써서 차
   자오기 힘드셜쪼?]

여자: 네. 제가 길치인 데다가 홍대를 처음 와서 찾기 어
   렵더라고요.

   [네, 제가 길치인 데다가 홍대를 처음 와서 찯끼 어
   렵떠라고요.]

Lesson 27

Section I - Vocabulary

1. e	2. a	3. g	4. i	5. f
6. c	7. b	8. d	9. j	10. h

Section II - Translation Practice

11. 재미있게 공부하기만 하면 or 재미있게 공부하는 한
12. 제가 열쇠를 가지고 있는 한 or 제가 열쇠를 가지고 있
    기만 하면
13. 너무 덥지 않는 한 or 너무 덥지만 않으면
14. 깨지지만 않으면 or 깨지지 않는 한
15. 사람들이 너무 많이 오지만 않으면 or 사람들이 너무
    많이 오지 않는 한

Section III - Comprehension

16. 네. 비(가) 오지만 않으면 갈 거예요.

A: Are we going to the Han River tomorrow?
B: Yes. As long as it doesn't rain, we will go.

17. 네. 엄마랑 같이 있기만 하면 안 울어요.

A: The baby doesn't cry.
B: No. As long as he/she is with his/her mom, he/
   she doesn't cry.

18. 내가 살아 있는 한 절대 허락할 수 없다.

A: Mother, please allow us to get married.
B: As long as I'm alive, I can't allow it.

19. 얼음물처럼 차갑지 않는 한 괜찮아요. 주세요.

A: The water is too cold. Will you be okay with it?
B: As long as it's not as cold as ice water, I'm fine.
   Please give me some.

20. 그래서 교수님이 시간 안에 제출하기만 하면 좋은 점
    수 주신다고 하셨어요.

A: The assignment this time is too difficult.
B: That's why the professor said that he/she would
   give us good grades as long as we submit it in
   time.

Section IV - Dictation

21. <u>너무 춥지만 않으면</u> 이번 주 수요일에 수영장에 갈 거
    예요.

   (= As long as it's not too cold, I'm going to go to a
   swimming pool this Wednesday.)

22. <u>약속을 지키기만 하면</u> 문제 없을 거예요.

   (= As long as you keep the promise, there will be
   no problem.)

<Transcript>

여자: 잘 데가 이 소파밖에 없는데 어떡하죠?

남자: 괜찮아요. 저는 아무 데나 눕기만 하면 자요.

여자: 불편할 것 같아서요.

남자: 괜찮다니까요. 너무 춥지만 않으면 푹 잘 수 있어
요. 여기 춥지는 않죠?

여자: 네. 창문을 열고 자지 않는 한 안 추울 거예요.

Woman: There's nowhere to sleep but this sofa.
What should we do?

Man: It's fine. I sleep anywhere as long as I lie
down.

Woman: (I'm worried because) I think it will be
uncomfortable.

Man: I said it's fine. As long as it is not too cold, I
can sleep well. It's not too cold here, right?

Woman: No. As long as you don't sleep with the
window open, it's not going to be cold.

23.
• Correct statements: a
• Incorrect statements: b, c, d

Section VI - Speaking Practice

여자: 잘 데가 이 소파밖에 없는데 어떡하죠?

  [잘 떼가 이 소파바께 엄는데 어떠카조?]

남자: 괜찮아요.

  [괜차나요.]

  저는 아무 데나 눕기만 하면 자요.

  [저는 아무 데나 눕끼만 하면 자요.]

여자: 불편할 것 같아서요.

  [불편할 껃 가타서요.]

남자: 괜찮다니까요.

  [괜찬타니까요.]

  너무 춥지만 않으면 푹 잘 수 있어요.

  [너무 춥찌만 아느면 푹 쑤 이써요.]

  여기 춥지는 않죠?

  [여기 춥찌는 안초?]

여자: 네. 창문을 열고 자지 않는 한 안 추울 거예요.

  [네. 창무늘 열고 자지 안는 한 안 추울 꺼예요.]

Lesson 28

Section I - Vocabulary

1. i	2. h	3. e	4. d	5. j
6. c	7. a	8. g	9. f	10. b

Section II - Complete the Sentence

11. 혼자 보낸다는 것은 외로운 일이에요

12. 직업으로 갖는다는 것은 스트레스받는 일이에요

13. 혼자 공부한다는 것은 쉽지 않은 일이에요

14. 시험을 본다는 것은 무모한 일이에요

15. 휴가를 쓴다는 것은 대단한 일이에요

Section III - Translation Practice

16. 배운다는 것

17. 외국에 산다는 것

18. 아이를 키운다는 것

19. 한국에서 유명한 가수가 된다는 것

20. 장학금을 받는다는 것

Section IV - Dictation

21. 주말에도 <u>회사에 가야 한다는 건</u> 정말 슬픈 일이에요.

  (= Having to go to work on the weekend is so
  sad.)

22. <u>엄마가 된다는 건</u> 아름다운 일이에요.

  (= Becoming a mother is a beautiful thing.)

Section V - Listening Comprehension

<Transcript>

여자: 이 영화는 제가 정말 좋아하는 영화예요.

남자: 어떤 내용인데요?

여자: '아버지가 된다는 것은 무엇일까?'라고 물어보
는 영화예요.

남자: 오! 재밌을 것 같네요. 요즘 가족이 된다는 것이

Talk To Me In Korean Workbook

어떤 의미인지에 대해서 이야기하는 영화가 많은 것 같아요.

Woman: This movie is the movie that I really like.

Man: What is it about?

Woman: It's the movie that asks, "What would it be like to become a father?"

Man: Oh, that sounds fun. It seems that there are a lot of movies that talk about what becoming a family means these days.

23. b

Section VI - Speaking Practice

여자: 이 영화는 제가 정말 좋아하는 영화예요.

   [이 영화는 제가 정말 조아하는 영화예요.]

남자: 어떤 내용인데요?

   [어떤 내용인데요?]

여자: '아버지가 된다는 것은 무엇일까?'라고 물어보는 영화예요.

   ['아버지가 된다는 거슨 무어실까?'라고 무러보는 영화예요.]

남자: 오! 재밌을 것 같네요.

   [오! 재미쓸 껃 간네요.]

   요즘 가족이 된다는 것이 어떤 의미인지에 대해서 이야기하는 영화가 많은 것 같아요.

   [요즘 가조기 된다는 거시 어떤 의미인지에 대해서 이야기하는 영화가 마는 걷 가타요.]

Lesson 29

Section I - Vocabulary

1. e   2. a   3. g   4. b   5. d

6. c   7. h   8. i   9. j   10. f

Section II - Translation Practice

11. 늦지 않도록

12. 넘어지지 않도록

13. 뒤에서도 볼 수 있도록 or 뒤에서도 보이도록

14. 제가 이해할 수 있도록

15. 뒤에 있는 사람들도 들을 수 있도록

Section III - Complete the Dialogue

16. 배가 터지도록 먹었어요

17. 노래가 너무 좋아서 질리도록 들었어요

18. 사람들이 지나갈 수 있도록

19. 입이 아프도록

20. 학생들이 이해하기 쉽도록

Section IV - Dictation

21. 이 신발은 다 떨어지도록 자주 신었어요.

   (= I've worn these shoes so often, almost to the point where they are worn out.)

22. 요즘 밤늦도록 일하느라고 잠을 잘 못 잤어요.

   (= I've been working late these days, so I haven't been able to sleep enough.)

Section V - Listening Comprehension

<Transcript>

여자: 요즘 잠을 못 자서 너무 피곤해요.

남자: 왜 잠을 못 잤어요?

여자: 매일 밤늦도록 일하느라고요.

남자: 힘내요. 내일 주말이잖아요. 주말에 질리도록 자요.

Woman: I'm so tired because I can't sleep these days.

Man: Why couldn't you sleep?

Woman: Because I was working late into the night every day.

Man: Cheer up. Tomorrow is the weekend, isn't it? During the weekend, sleep to the point where you get sick of sleeping.

23. c

Section VI - Speaking Practice

여자: 요즘 잠을 못 자서 너무 피곤해요.

   [요즘 자믈 몯 짜서 너무 피곤해요.]

남자: 왜 잠을 못 잤어요?

　　　[왜 자믈 몯 짜써요?]

여자: 매일 밤늦도록 일하느라고요.

　　　[매일 밤늗또록 일하느라고요.]

남자: 힘내요.

　　　[힘내요.]

　　　내일 주말이잖아요.

　　　[내일 주마리자나요.]

　　　주말에 질리도록 자요.

　　　[주마레 질리도록 자요.]

Lesson 30

Section I - Vocabulary

1. a	2. h	3. i	4. e	5. j
6. d	7. c	8. f	9. g	10. b

Section II - Matching

11. 직원들한테 물어보나 마나 제 말에 동의한다고 할 거예요.

　　(= Even if you ask your/my employees, they will say that they agree with me.)

12. 영상을 꾸준히 올리기만 하면 구독자들이 생기게 되어 있어요.

　　(= As long as you upload videos regularly, you are bound to have subscribers.)

13. 저희 팀은 일도 잘하는 데다가 분위기도 좋은 편이에요.

　　(= On top of being good at what we do, the atmosphere is also pretty nice in my team.)

14. 그 음식은 굉장히 짠 데다가 맵기도 해요.

　　(= On top of being really salty, the food is also spicy.)

15. 밥을 주나 마나 또 배고프다고 할 거예요.

　　(= Regardless of whether you give him/her food or not, they will say they are hungry again.)

16. 덜 먹고 열심히 운동하기만 하면 살이 빠지게 되어 있어요.

　　(= As long as you eat less and exercise hard, you are bound to lose weight.)

17. 중간에 공부를 포기하지만 않으면 좋은 결과를 얻게 되어 있어요.

　　(= As long as you don't give up studying in the middle, you are bound to get good results.)

18. 그 컴퓨터는 너무 느린 데다가 소리도 크게 나는 편이에요.

　　(= On top of being too slow, the computer also makes quite loud noises.)

Section III - Reading Comprehension

\<Translation\>

Hello! I am a college student living in Korea called Jina.

I have been having a crush on my friend, Seokjin, for five years. We have been friends since we were high school students. Seokjin is handsome, and on top of that, he is pretty tall. Also, we have similar personalities, and we are good conversation partners. That was why I came to like Seokjin.

My friends say that I should confess my feelings to Seokjin. However, I don't think it will work well whether I confess or not. I don't think Seokjin likes me. As long as I don't confess, Seokjin and I will be able to stay friends. However, if I confess, maybe we might not be able to stay friends, right? That is my concern. Do you still think giving confession a go is better than not doing it?

Thank you for reading my story.

19. c

20. 성격도 저랑 잘 맞는 데다가, 대화도 잘 통하는 편이에요.

Section IV - Dictation

21. <u>확인해 보나 마나</u> 바쁘다고 할 거예요.

　　(= Whether you check or not, they will say that they are busy.)

22. 여기는 날씨도 추운 데다가 물가도 비싼 편이에요.

   (= On top of being cold here, the prices are
   rather high too.)

Section V - Listening Comprehension

<Transcript>

여자: 내일 아침 비행기는 보나 마나 결항될 것 같아요.

남자: 아니에요. 바람이 많이 불지만 않으면 비행기 뜰
      수 있대요.

여자: 아, 정말요?

남자: 네. 그래서 비 오는 날보다 바람 많이 부는 날 결
      항이 더 자주 되는 편이에요.

Woman: I think flights for tomorrow morning will
         be canceled without a doubt.

Man: No, they won't. As long as it isn't too windy, I
      heard that planes can take off.

Woman: Oh, really?

Man: Yes. Therefore, flights get canceled more
      often on a windy day than on a rainy day.

23. c

Section VI - Speaking Practice

여자: 내일 아침 비행기는 보나 마나 결항될 것 같아요.
      [내일 아침 비행기는 보나 마나 결항될 껄 가타요.]

남자: 아니에요.
      [아니에요.]
      바람이 많이 불지만 않으면 비행기 뜰 수 있대요.
      [바라미 마니 불지만 아느면 비행기 뜰 쑤 읻때요.]

여자: 아, 정말요?
      [아, 정마료?]

남자: 네. 그래서 비 오는 날보다 바람 많이 부는 날 결항
      이 더 자주 되는 편이에요.
      [네. 그래서 비 오는 날보다 바람 마니 부는 날 결항
      이 더 자주 되는 펴니에요.]

iOS   Android

TTMIK Book Audio App

Download our app TTMIK: Audio to listen to all the
book audio tracks conveniently on your phone!
The app is available for free on both iOS and
Android. Search for TTMIK: Audio in your app store.

Learn More Effectively with Our Premium Courses

Gain unlimited access to hundreds of video and audio lessons by becoming
a Premium Member on our website, https://talktomeinkorean.com!

Bibimchat: One-stop Korean Listening Source

▶ 37

Added ✓

Long Sentence Training

▶ 10

Added ✓

IYAGI (intermediate) ~ Listening in 100% Natural Korean

🎧 145

Added ✓